Troy Glaus

and the ANAHEIM ANGELS

2002 WORLD SERIES

by Michael Sandler

Consultant: Jim Sherman
Head Baseball Coach
University of Delaware

BEARPORT
PUBLISHING

New York, New York

Credits

Cover and Title Page, © Robert Laberge/Getty Images; 4, © Contra Costa Times/ZUMA Press/Icon SMI; 5, © Lucy Nicholson/AFP/Getty Images; 6, © David Young-Wolf/PhotEdit; 7, © Christian Petersen/Getty Images; 8, © VJ Lovero/Sports Illustrated; 10, © Jed Jacobsohn/Getty Images; 11, © Allsport USA/ Allsport/Getty Images; 12, © AP Images/ Chris Urso; 13, © Stephen Dunn/Getty Images; 14, © Timothy A Clary/AFP/Getty Images; 15, © John Cordes/Icon SMI; 16, © Monica Davey/AFP/Getty Images; 17, © Jeff Gross/ Getty Images; 18, © Al Bello/Getty Images; 19, © REUTERS/Dave Kennedy; 20, © Donald Miralle/Getty Images; 21, © Brian Bahr/Getty Images; 22T, © John Cordes/Icon SMI; 22C, © REUTERS/Mike Segar; 22B, © Jeff Haynes/AFP/Getty Images.

Publisher: Kenn Goin
Senior Editor: Lisa Wiseman
Creative Director: Spencer Brinker
Design: Stacey May
Photo Researcher: Omni-Photo Communications, Inc.

Library of Congress Cataloging-in-Publication Data

Sandler, Michael.
 Troy Glaus and the Anaheim Angels : 2002 World Series / by Michael Sandler.
     p. cm. — (World Series superstars)
 Includes bibliographical references and index.
 ISBN-13: 978-1-59716-640-9 (library binding)
 ISBN-10: 1-59716-640-5 (library binding)
 1. Glaus, Troy—Juvenile literature. 2. Baseball players—United States—Biography—Juvenile literature. 3. Anaheim Angels (Baseball team)—Juvenile literature. 4. World Series (Baseball) (2002) —Juvenile literature. I. Title.

 GV865.G53 S36
 796.357092—dc22
 (B)

                    2007032668

For more information, write to Bearport Publishing Company, Inc., 101 Fifth Avenue, Suite 6R, New York, New York 10003. Printed in the United States of America.

10 9 8 7 6 5 4 3 2 1

★ Contents ★

Now or Never

Troy Glaus knew his team was running out of time. Six more outs and the Angels would lose the 2002 World Series to the San Francisco Giants.

Up in the stands, Angels fans were counting on Troy. Could he get them the hit they needed? Could he bring the runners home and force a Game 7?

Down in the **batter's box**, Troy waited for the pitch.

Angels fans root for their team.

Troy about to hit the ball during the 2002 World Series

Throughout their history, the Angels have changed their team name many times. Today, they are known as the Los Angeles Angels of Anaheim.

Hometown Hitter

For Troy, being an Angel was a dream come true. He had always wanted to be a baseball player. He had grown up in Southern California where the Angels play. He loved going to the park to watch their games.

Troy's mom tried to help him reach his goal. As a working single mother, she didn't have much free time. Still, when she had a chance, she helped her son practice hitting.

Troy was born in Tarzana, California.

The home of the
Anaheim Angels

Troy's mom ran a trucking
business. As a kid, Troy loved
to play in the huge trucks she
parked in the driveway.

Making It to the Majors

All Troy's practice paid off. He became a big-hitting high school player. Then he went on to become a college baseball star at UCLA. In 1997, he was **drafted** by the Angels.

The young third baseman quickly became known as a home-run hitter. In his first three full seasons, he smashed 117 homers. In both 2000 and 2001, he earned a place in the **All-Star Game**.

Troy played on the 1996 U.S. Olympic baseball team.

In 2000, Troy led the **American League** in home runs. His 47 homers were an Angels record.

Troy's rookie baseball card

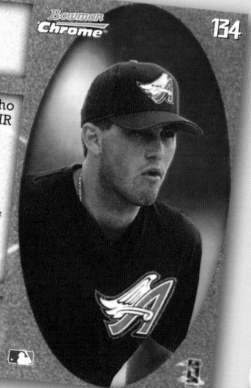

TROY GLAUS

HT: 6'5" WT: 215 BATS: RIGHT THROWS: RIGHT
BORN: 8-3-76, TARZANA, CA
DRAFTED: ANGELS #1-JUNE, 1997 ACQ: VIA DRAFT

Bowman Chrome 134

Scouting Report

RESUME: Third overall draft pick in 1997 who will make pro debut in '98...All-time UCLA HR leader for season (34, '97) and career (62)... Was Pac-10 Player of the Year after batting .409 with 91 RBI in 67 games...'96 Olympian.

SKILLS: Gifted hitter...Will use the whole yard...Gets under the ball and hits it a long way...Won't clog the bases...Prototype actions at 3B...Major League arm.

UP CLOSE: HR'd in UCLA-record 5 straight games as sophomore.

Minor League Batting Record

	G	AB	HR	RBI	AVG	SLG
1997			DID NOT PLAY			
CAREER TOTALS	1998 WILL BE FIRST PROFESSIONAL SEASON					

Hard-Luck Team

For Angels fans, Troy's success was a bright spot. Often, the team gave them little to cheer about.

In its 40-year history, the Angels had never won a World Series. In fact, the team had never even played in one.

Whenever the Angels came close, something happened—injuries, bad luck, or better **opponents**. Being an Angels fan wasn't easy.

Though they were often disappointed, Angels fans always cheered on their team.

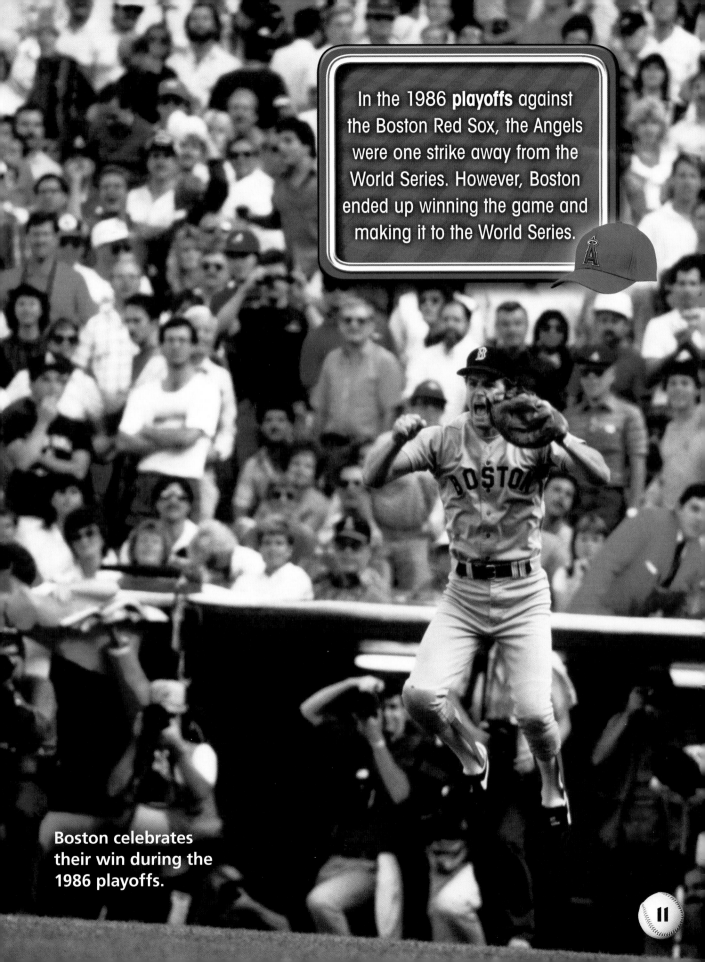

In the 1986 **playoffs** against the Boston Red Sox, the Angels were one strike away from the World Series. However, Boston ended up winning the game and making it to the World Series.

Boston celebrates their win during the 1986 playoffs.

Turning It Around

At first, the 2002 season seemed like it would be another tough one. The Angels lost 14 of their first 20 games. Even Troy struggled at the plate.

In late summer, however, the Angels went on a roll. They won 16 out of 17 games to grab the **division** lead. Though they couldn't hold on to first place, they did gain a **wild-card playoff spot**.

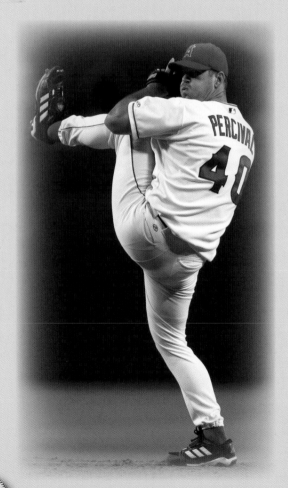

Relief pitcher Troy Percival helped the Angels win many games in 2002.

Troy at bat during a game against the Oakland A's in 2002

On September 15, 2002, Troy hit three home runs in a game to put Anaheim in first place.

Playoff Push

First up in the playoffs were the New York Yankees. Though the powerful Yankees were expected to win, the Angels took the series easily.

Next, the Angels played the Minnesota Twins. The Twins won the first game, but then the Angels took over. Troy led the way with one big hit after another.

For the first time ever, Troy's hometown Angels were headed to a World Series. There they would face another California team, the San Francisco Giants.

The Twins were not happy losing to the Angels.

The Angels enjoy their win.

No **major-league** team had been around as long as the Angels without reaching the World Series at least once.

Battling Barry

The Giants' biggest weapon was **slugger** Barry Bonds, one of baseball's most feared hitters. Just two innings into Game 1, Barry hit his first homer.

Troy tried to bring the Angels back into the game. In the second inning, he sent a pitch sailing over the left-field fence. Then, in the sixth inning, he smashed another home run.

With Troy and Barry trading homers, the series went back and forth. After five games, the Giants led the series, 3-2.

Troy rounds the bases after hitting a home run against the Giants.

Barry Bonds hit the ball out of the stadium during the second inning of Game 1.

Barry is Major League Baseball's all-time home run king. On August 7, 2007, he broke Hank Aaron's career record of 755 homers.

Game 6

For Anaheim, winning Game 6 was a must. Yet with the series on the line, they quickly fell behind. The Giants got ready to celebrate.

Once again, Troy didn't give up. His seventh-inning single sparked a three-run **rally**. The Angels were back in the game!

In the eighth inning, they scored again. The Giants were now only ahead by one run. Troy came to the plate with two Angels on base. Could he bring them home to give Anaheim the lead?

Kenny Lofton slides safely into base, helping the Giants take an early lead in Game 6.

Troy at bat in the eighth inning

The Angels were down by five runs in the seventh inning of Game 6. No team facing World Series **elimination** had ever come back after being down so much.

Champions at Last

Troy hit the ball deep. In left center field, Barry Bonds ran after it. Could he reach it? No! The Angels' runners came home to score.

The two runs gave Anaheim a stunning 6-5 victory. The series was tied. Troy's hit had forced a **winner-take-all** seventh game.

In Game 7, Angels pitcher John Lackey took over. He gave up just one run as Anaheim rolled to an easy 4-1 victory. Troy and the Angels had finally won a World Series!

The Anaheim Angels celebrate their Game 6 win.

After the game, Troy was named **MVP** of the 2002 World Series.

Key Players

Troy, along with some other key players, helped the Anaheim Angels win the 2002 World Series.

Troy Glaus #25

Third Base

Bats: Right   Throws: Right
Born: 8/3/1976 in Tarzana, California
Height: 6'5" (1.96 m)
Weight: 240 pounds (109 kg)

Series Highlights
Hit a double to give the Angels a Game 6 win; hit three home runs during the series

John Lackey #41

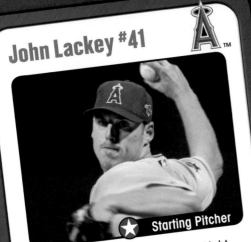

Starting Pitcher

Bats: Right   Throws: Right
Born: 10/23/1978 in Abilene, Texas
Height: 6'6" (1.98 m)
Weight: 245 pounds (111 kg)

Series Highlight
Pitched the Angels to a Game 7 win

Garret Anderson #16

Left Field

Bats: Left   Throws: Left
Born: 6/30/1972 in Los Angeles, California
Height: 6'3" (1.90 m)
Weight: 225 pounds (102 kg)

Series Highlight
Drove home three runs with a double during Game 7

★ Glossary ★

All-Star Game (AWL-STAR GAME) a yearly game between the National and American leagues; only the best players in each league are chosen to play

American League (uh-MER-uh-kuhn LEEG) one of the two major professional baseball leagues in the United States

batter's box (BAT-urz BOKS) the place where a batter stands at home plate while waiting to hit a pitch

division (di-VIZH-uhn) a group of teams that compete against one another for a playoff spot

drafted (DRAFT-id) picked to play for a professional team

elimination (i-*lim*-uh-NAY-shuhn) when a team is removed from the playoffs after losing

major league (MAY-jur LEEG) the highest level of professional baseball in the United States, made up of the American League and the National League

MVP (EM-VEE-PEE) the most valuable player in a game or season

opponents (uh-POH-nuhnts) teams or athletes who others play against in a sporting event

playoffs (PLAY-awfss) games held after the regular season to determine who will play in the World Series

rally (RA-lee) when a team comes back in a game after being far behind

slugger (SLUHG-er) a player who often hits doubles, triples, and home runs

wild-card playoff spot (WILDE-kard PLAY-awf SPOT) a playoff spot for a team that did not win its division

winner-take-all (WIN-ur-TAYK-AWL) a single game that decides which team will win a series

Bibliography

Newhan, Ross. *Anaheim Angels: A Complete History.* New York: Hyperion (2000).

Verducci, Tom. "Troy Story." *Sports Illustrated* (June 12, 2000).

Baseball Digest

The New York Times

Read More

Clendening, John. *American League West.* Mankato, MN: Child's World (2005).

Gilbert, Sarah. *The Story of the Los Angeles Angels.* Mankato, MN: Creative Education (2007).

Stewart, Mark. *The Los Angeles Angels of Anaheim.* Chicago: Norwood House Press (2006).

Learn More Online

To learn more about Troy Glaus,
the Anaheim Angels, and the World Series, visit
www.bearportpublishing.com/WorldSeriesSuperstars

Index

The Illustrated
TIGERS OF INDIA

The Oxford India Collection is a series which brings together
writings of enduring value published by OUP.

Other titles include

The Oxford India Illustrated Corbett
The Second Oxford India Illustrated Corbett
The Oxford India Illustrated Children's Tagore
The Illustrated Premchand: Selected Short Stories
The Illustrated Sálim Ali: The Fall of a Sparrow

The Illustrated
TIGERS OF INDIA

Valmik Thapar

UNIVERSITY PRESS

OXFORD
UNIVERSITY PRESS

YMCA Library Building, Jai Singh Road, New Delhi 110 001

Oxford University Press is a department of the University of Oxford.
It furthers the University's objective of excellence in research, scholarship,
and education by publishing worldwide in

Oxford   New York
Auckland   Cape Town   Dar es Salaam   Hong Kong   Karachi
Kuala Lumpur   Madrid   Melbourne   Mexico City   Nairobi
New Delhi   Shanghai   Taipei   Toronto

With offices in
Argentina   Austria   Brazil   Chile   Czech Republic   France   Greece
Guatemala   Hungary   Italy   Japan   Poland   Portugal   Singapore
South Korea   Switzerland   Thailand   Turkey   Ukraine   Vietnam

Oxford is a registered trade mark of Oxford University Press
in the UK and in certain other countries.

Published in India by Oxford University Press, New Delhi

Oxford University Press India would like to thank K. Ullas Karanth, M. Monirul H. Khan,
and Fateh Singh Rathore for giving permission to use selections from their writings,
and Amit Sankhala for giving permission to use extracts from his grandfather
Kailash Sankhala's book *Tiger! The Story of the Indian Tiger*

Illustrations by Kallol Majumder
Photographs of tiger cubs (by Bittu Sahgal), tiger swimming across a waterway in
the Sundarbans (by K.M. Narayana Swamy), and two tigers watching a gaur
(by Sudhir Shivaram) in the colour section courtesy Sanctuary Photo Library

ISBN-13: 978-0-19-569170-2
ISBN-10: 0-19-569170-9

Typeset in Lapidary333 BT 12.5/15.5
by Eleven Arts, Keshav Puram, Delhi 110 035
Printed in India by Thomson Press (India) Ltd., New Delhi 110 020
Published by Oxford University Press
YMCA Library Building, Jai Singh Road, New Delhi 110 00

Contents

For my son Hamir

Author's Note

Why another book on the tiger? Because it is vital in this severe crisis to make civil society and the public at large aware of the state of affairs. It is essential for people to read about this majestic predator that roamed the length and breadth of India. Can we let it go? Or is it worth a fight? Let's find out in this affordable book by the Oxford University Press which provides in its pages a comprehensive reference for 'everything you wanted to know' about the tiger in India. It puts together, simplifies, and abridges information from many of my previous books, especially *Tiger: The Ultimate Guide*, in order to engage a larger audience with the subject of the book—the tiger.

It is people from all walks of life who have to come together in the battle to save the tiger, and I hope this book plays a part in this endeavour. Let's not forget that this nation has seen leaders like Jawaharlal Nehru, Indira Gandhi, and Rajiv Gandhi who spoke up for the wilderness. It is the public at large that must force today's leaders to do the same.

I must thank the editors at Oxford University Press for their detailed assistance in putting the book together. I would also like to thank Kallol Majumder for the evocative illustrations he has done for the book, and Bittu Sahgal, K.M. Narayana Swamy, Sudhir Shivaram, and Ashish Kothari for giving permission to use their photographs in the book.

Valmik Thapar

Publisher's Note

The tiger in India is today an endangered species with its numbers dwindling alarmingly. With more and more forest area being cleared for 'civilization' and with the high value of tiger skin and parts in Tibetan ceremonial costumes and Chinese medicine, tigers are fast disappearing from the face of this land. In this situation the voices of Valmik Thapar, one of our foremost tiger conservationists, and others like him are isolated voices in the wilderness. Disillusioned with the official speak, he argues that the tiger has a future in this country only if people come together and battle for its survival.

It is towards this end that the Oxford University Press presents this unique volume where many of Thapar's earlier writings and new materials—accessible and accompanied by breathtaking yet realistic visuals—are presented to engage a wider audience, especially young readers with the future of this magnificent animal. *The Illustrated Tigers of India*, part of the Oxford India Illustrated Collection which brings together writings of enduring value, is thus both comprehensive yet highly accessible providing lay readers a one-stop reference on the tiger in India.

The narrative tracks the story of the tiger from its origins to the present day. The 'Tiger Factsheet' provides interesting tiger facts and other details in an imaginative and simple way, and the 'Tiger Map' locates its presence in different parts of India. The book tracks the tiger from birth through adulthood through firsthand accounts of tigers in the wild, largely by Thapar himself, and also by other tiger experts, past and present, most notably A.A. Dunbar Brander, Jim Corbett, Kailash Sankhala, K. Ullas Karanth, M. Monirul H. Khan, and Fateh Singh Rathore. Thus anecdote and incident enliven biological phenomena. The whole is complemented by photographs and illustrations that are both authentic and rare. Readers get to view a tigress with her cubs, playful siblings learning to hunt, the father with his young family, as also adult tigers on the hunt and with a variety of prey ranging from the small peafowl to the mammoth gaur. The colour section, a special feature of the volume, depicts the life cycle of the tiger.

If we are to save this precious heritage of ours from extinction, we have to overcome our apathy and act now. Thapar makes an impassioned appeal for drastic measures to at least halt, if not reverse, the damage. Innovative and out-of-the-box remedies are required feels Thapar, who suggests shifting tigers from locations that are too close to human habitation to relatively more protected and secure areas. Saving the tiger and his immediate environment is saving India's wildlife and our environment. Creating awareness about the tiger and its crises is the first set. We hope this book will engage and inform readers to step forward to save the tiger.

The Illustrated
TIGERS OF INDIA

Introducing the Tiger

The Origins of the Tiger

Zoologists and other animal experts call the majestic striped big cat commonly known as the tiger, *Panthera tigris*. *Panthera* is the name given to the genus (group) of the four big cats in the world that have the ability to roar with spine-chilling effect: the tiger, lion, leopard, and jaguar, although technically tigers do not roar in the same way as lions and leopards do. The snow leopard has sometimes been classed as *Panthera*, although nowadays it is placed in its own genus, *Uncia*, and is believed to have diverged from *Panthera* about four million years ago. Roaring is made possible by the vibration of thickened vocal folds just below the vocal cords in the larynx. Snow leopards have less well-developed vocal folds and are thus not quite *Panthera*, whereas the smaller cats, which can only purr and scream, have narrow vocal folds. *Tigris*—the species name that differentiates the tiger from the other members of the genus, *Panthera leo* (lion), *Panthera pardus* (leopard), and *Panthera onca* (jaguar)—is classical Greek for 'arrow', from which both the straight and fast-flowing river Tigris and the speedy tiger get their names.

The Tiger through the Ages

The origins of the tiger trace back some fifty million years, long before anything recognizable as today's big cats existed. Fossils provide most of the evidence scientists and researchers have used to piece together our understanding of the emergence of the tiger.

The oldest tiger ancestors were mammals called miacids, the first true carnivores, which crept around in the treetops and who appeared fifty million years ago. They were not spectacular to look at, just small, long tree climbers, a bit like pine martens today.

The Pseudaelurines, a group of cats that first appear in the fossil record about twenty million years ago, are thought to be the direct ancestors of today's thirty-seven species of cat, including the tiger. The oldest cat, *Proailurus*, came from what we now call France about thirty million years ago. It was about the same size as and probably had an arboreal lifestyle similar to that of the fossa of Madagascar, which is closely related to mongooses, but in isolation and in the absence of competing cats it evolved a catlike morphology. *Proailurus* had eight more teeth than today's cats.

It is thought that more than two million years ago the common ancestor to the *Panthera* cats was fairly similar to the modern leopard in looks. Using molecular techniques to compare the genetic similarities among the modern-day members of the *Panthera* genus, zoologists have determined that the tiger diverged first from the common *Panthera* ancestor and that the lion, leopard, and jaguar evolved much later.

About two million years ago, our ancestor, *Homo habilis*, began to evolve into *Homo erectus* and eventually dispersed out of Africa and migrated as far as China. *Homo sapiens*, the species to which all modern humans belong, did not appear until about four hundred thousand years ago.

Miacids are an extinct group of carnivores that gave rise to dogs, bears, skunks, mongooses, cats, and hyenas.

Early tiger fossils (one to two million years old) have been found in China, Java, and Sumatra. The earliest in Russia are only seven hundred thousand years old, and those in India are only ten thousand years old. Recent fossil and other evidence suggests that tigers existed in Borneo, perhaps even as recently as a few hundred years ago.

From this scant fossil record, scientists have come up with two alternative theories. The most accepted version, the Asian theory, asserts that more than two million years ago, when early man had yet to venture out of Africa, tigers separated from their big cat cousins in East Asia, with the South China form being the original template. These tigers dispersed two million years ago in two directions, one group travelling north to Russia while the second spread south-east to the Indonesian islands and south-west to India.

Around twelve thousand years ago (or ten thousand radiocarbon years), mastodons, mammoths, woolly rhinoceroses, and other megafauna became extinct, and the last major ice age, which had covered Britain in ice as far south as Oxford, ended. As the land became warmer, trees grew, creating forests across Britain. European lions, which had been common for nine hundred thousand years, became extinct. The Sahara had higher rainfall and became habitable. Mehrgarh, one of the oldest cities in the world, was founded about this time in the Indus Valley. In North America, sabre-toothed cats and the American lion were nearing the end of their lengthy carnivorous reigns and were becoming extinct. Fossils discovered at Karnool cave deposits in Andhra Pradesh tell us that this is the period when tigers first entered India.

The peoples of the Indus Valley civilization of Harappa and Mohenjo Daro (part of modern Pakistan) were the first to use the tiger as an important symbol in their cultures, engraved on seals that are believed to have marked ownership of property and that were worn as amulets.

Around two thousand years ago, the Roman Empire was at its peak. Use of Caspian tigers in the games and slaughters in amphitheatres introduced the first significant threat to the tiger's existence. One thousand years ago, Europe entered the Dark Ages, and Asia (excluding

SABRE-TOOTHED CATS

Despite their name, the famous sabre-toothed cats are probably not ancestors of today's tigers at all. They are distant relatives who used terrifyingly long and specialized 'sabre' teeth to kill their prey.

The most famous of the sabre-toothed cats is *Smilodon*, well known because of the huge number of fossils found in the Rancho La Brea tar pits in Hollywood, California. We know that it lived from about 1.5 million years ago to 120,000 years ago and was an awesome predator about 1.2 m long (similar in size to an African lion), with a bobbed tail. It was *Smilodon's* jaws that made it stand out in the crowd; they were huge, opening to an angle of more than 90 degrees (today's lions can open their jaws only to 65 degrees), which made it easy to sink their 18 cm canine teeth into prey. Surprisingly, these sabres were quite delicate—any contact with bone would shatter them, so they could be used only in the soft parts of the prey such as the underbelly and throat. *Smilodon* therefore needed strong front legs to hold its victim still and very sharp claws to help it hang on during hunting.

The sabre-toothed cats died out probably in large part because of their lack of adaptability in hunting techniques, although hunting pressure from early humans and competition from pantherine species such as the lion may also have contributed to their demise.

Japan) accounted for two-thirds of world gross domestic product. Western Europe was in its infancy.

The earth as a whole was warmer, and wild boars, beavers, and wolves still roamed the diminishing forests of Britain. With people far less numerous and lethal than they are now, tiger populations maintained an equilibrium and enjoyed wide distribution.

With his arms outstretched, a warrior fends off a pair of tigers on this Mohenjo Daro seal of the Indus Valley civilization, 3000 to 1700 BCE.

The tiger population suffered unprecedented decimation when the proliferation of firearms and cars from two hundred to one hundred years ago facilitated hunting for sport or purely medicinal purposes. People also hunted the tiger's prey, leaving tigers with less and less to eat. Humankind encroached upon the tiger's natural habitats, converting them to agricultural lands.

In the fifty years between 1875 and 1925, eighty thousand tigers were killed in India alone. Probably an equal number were injured and died later of their wounds. Based on these and other figures, it is conservatively estimated that at the dawn of the twentieth century one hundred thousand tigers inhabited the range from eastern Turkey across the Asian continent to the Russian Far East and the islands of Indonesia.

Tigers Today

Today there are an estimated five thousand to seven thousand tigers living in the wild, spanning eighteen countries, from the snowy Russian Far East to the dense sweltering jungles of Sumatra. Tigers are incredibly versatile animals, living in temperatures that range from −33°C (−28°F) in the northern extreme of their range to 50°C (122°F) in the southern parts, and altitudes ranging from sea level to more than 3000 m. Not only do temperature and altitude vary greatly, so, of course, does vegetation, from the tropical evergreen and deciduous forests of southern Asia to the coniferous, scrub oak, and

A typical big game hunting expedition. A cornered tiger attacks the elephant and gets shot at close range.

birch woodlands of Siberia. Tigers also thrive in the mangrove swamps of the Sundarbans, the dry thorn forests of north-western India, and the tall grass jungles at the foot of the Himalayas. They need only dense vegetative cover, sufficient large ungulate prey, and access to water to survive.

Tiger Subspecies

Within any given subspecies, there is variation in size and colouring from individual to individual, and there is often overlap in morphology between subspecies, but the tiger has adapted to cope with the different habitats, climates, and available prey. The most northerly animals are generally larger, paler, and have thick, shaggy coats to cope with the cold, while the southern animals, which live in dense jungle and intense heat, are smaller, darker, and have shorter fur.

Until recently, tigers were divided into eight subspecies, often with country-specific names. Andrew Kitchener pioneered the research that led to the reduction in the number of tiger subspecies from eight to five. The Caspian, Javan, and Bali tigers are today extinct.

There are only about 400–600 Sumatra tigers left. Recent estimates of the Indo-Chinese tigers range between 1500 and 1800. The Chinese or South China tiger was once plentiful in parts of China but today there are only 30–40 left. The largest tiger is the Siberian tiger of which there are now around 400 left.

The Indian or Bengal tiger lives in India, Nepal, Bhutan, Bangladesh, and possibly parts of Burma (Myanmar). It can live over 4000 m up in the mountains of Bhutan or at the edge of the sea in the mangrove swamps of the Sundarbans in India. There are about 3000–4000 Bengal tigers alive today. This book is about the Bengal tiger—its anatomy, life cycle, family life, hunting skills, habits, and spread; its beauty, power, and influence; and, most of all, the very potent threat of extinction it faces today. Once worshipped because of its power, beauty, and the fear it inspired, in India and South Asia and in fact across all of Asia, the spread of firearms and explosion in human population with its hunger for agricultural and grazing land have left the tiger struggling for its very survival.

Tiger Factsheet

Tiger Anatomy

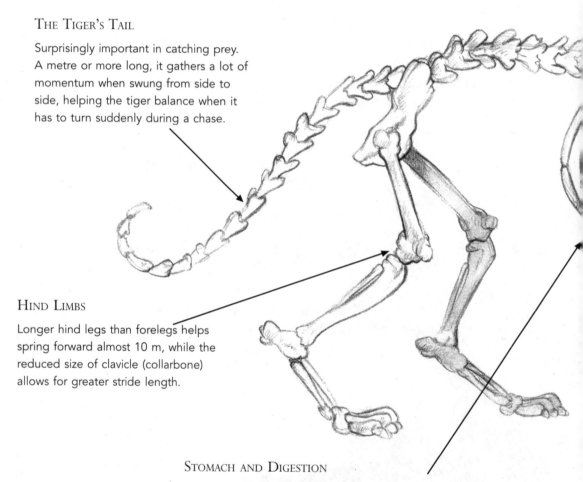

THE TIGER'S TAIL

Surprisingly important in catching prey.
A metre or more long, it gathers a lot of
momentum when swung from side to
side, helping the tiger balance when it
has to turn suddenly during a chase.

HIND LIMBS

Longer hind legs than forelegs helps
spring forward almost 10 m, while the
reduced size of clavicle (collarbone)
allows for greater stride length.

STOMACH AND DIGESTION

Shortened guts and comparatively small and light abdomens
(since it requires a far less complicated gut to convert meat to
protein, than it does to convert grass to protein) contribute to
its ability to accelerate quickly when in pursuit of prey.

Hair, Coat, or Pelage

The magnificent striping provides a perfect camouflage, but it functions primarily to keep the body warm and protect its skin. Tigers living in warmer southern latitudes have shorter fur (7–20 mm on the back and 15–35 mm on the stomach) than those in the colder northern habitats (40–60 mm on the back and 70–105 mm on the stomach, with as many as 3000 to 3300 hairs per sq cm).

maybe use this

Teeth

30 teeth, fewer than other carnivores (dogs and bears have 42) but no less dangerous, because of their specialization. Largest canines (6.4–7.6 cm long) among all the big cats. Canines are rich in pressure-sensitive nerves, enabling an accurate and deadly stab between a victim's neck bones to sever the spinal cord. Back teeth, called carnassials, act as shearing blades, which enable slicing the meat off the prey. Incisors (small front teeth) positioned in a straight line, help to efficiently pluck feathers and clean meat off the bone.

Fore Limbs

Solid forelimb bones (which can support large muscles) give the forelegs incredible power, enabling the tiger to bring down large prey.

Pads, Paws, and Claws

Claws (can be a fearsome 10 cm long) can take the face off a human in one swipe. Play a critical role in hunting: helping to grab and hold prey still until the teeth can inflict the final blow. There are four of these deadly weapons on each paw, with an extra dewclaw on the front ones.

Tiger Senses

THE SENSE OF TOUCH

Specialized hairs on the head known as whiskers, or vibrissae, serve a sensory function. Facial whiskers can be about 15 cm long, with those of males longer and heavier than those of females. Of all tigers, the Sunda Island subspecies *Panthera tigris sondaica* possesses the most generous number of whiskers.

THE SENSE OF TASTE

A large number of minute, sharp, backward-pointing projections known as papillae cover the tongues of tigers, giving them rough surfaces, which are used in conjunction with the teeth to remove feathers or fur from prey and to scrape particles of meat off bones when licking them.

THE SENSE OF SOUND

Most highly developed sense, far more important to the tiger's success as a hunter than either sight or smell. With large pinnae—external ear flaps—rotating like radar dishes, a tiger can catch many sounds and with experience determine precisely where they originated.

THE SENSE OF SMELL

Like other cats, tigers do not rely heavily on scent to find prey. Scent may not be the most important sense in hunting, but it is extremely important for the purposes of communication when a female is in estrus, say, or a rival male has been encroaching on another's territory.

THE SENSE OF SIGHT

Several special features increase the ability to see in the dark: large lenses and pupils receive more light; specially sensitive cells absorb the light; and reflective layers at the back of the retina (the light-sensitive cells at the back of the eye) give light more than one chance at stimulating light-receptor cells. Eyes work together to create a 3-D image (a phenomenon known as binocular vision)—a quality that is of huge importance in calculating how far away the prey is and then striking with accuracy.

Tiger Facts

Size

The tiger, whose proper nutrition depends upon consuming one deer-sized animal a week, has evolved into a supreme hunter. Male Bengal tigers can grow to 3.5 m, including the tail, and can weigh up to 200 kg. Females are smaller: up to about 2.6 m and between 100 and 160 kg.

Food

Tigers are at the top of their food chain. They hunt a wide range of animals—almost anything from birds such as peacocks to deer, young rhinos, snakes, and elephants. Near the sea, tigers even catch fish and crabs. However, large ungulate prey is generally their staple.

Lifecycle

Between one and seven cubs are born about fourteen weeks after the tigress mates with a male tiger. In the second month, the cubs start eating meat hunted by their mother and gradually they are weaned off their mother's milk altogether. From about eight to twenty months, the tigress teaches her cubs how to hunt. Between sixteen and twenty-four months, all the cubs have left their mother. Females are ready to have their first litter soon after they are three years old. Males tend to be ready to mate after four years. At five years they enter their prime. In the wild, tigers can live between twelve and sixteen years.

The Life of the Tiger

Throughout the centuries, when kings, emperors, and other rulers of the land went after the tiger with spears, guns, elephants, and hundreds of people in efforts to kill this 'striped devil', there was always a minority eager to keep forest habitats and wildlife alive. In the twentieth century, a few people began to take an interest in discovering something about the way the tiger lived, rather than focusing exclusively on how to kill it. In India, Major Jim Corbett, a legendary tiger hunter, and Frederick W. Champion, a forest officer, tried to photograph tigers with both still and movie cameras in an effort to understand more about them. In the 1920s and 1930s, little was known about the tiger save that it was solitary and evasive. Studying an elusive animal whose habits are unknown is difficult. Corbett may never have given up hunting, but he spent more and more time photographing tigers: he bought his first camera in the 1920s and filmed for more than twenty years. His major achievement was to get the provincial government in the foothills of the western Himalayas to create Hailey National Park in 1935, today a paradise for tigers called Corbett National Park.

The first serious information on tiger behaviour did not emerge until 1965, with the conclusion of a research project undertaken in central India by American zoologist George Schaller, who had already opened the eyes of the world to the behaviour of lions in the Serengeti. Now, for the first time, with the advent of some real 'tiger science', we began to understand facets of territorial behaviour and family life as never before.

By 1970, there was a complete ban on tiger shooting in India, and more and more areas were protected from development so that the tiger could live its life without fear of encroachment by mankind.

Until that time, tiger hunting had continued, with the result that tigers avoided people wherever they could, becoming nocturnal and never appearing unless attracted to bait—Schaller had relied heavily on the use of tethered buffalo to attract tigers to areas where they could be observed. While most of the world still believed that tigers were basically man-eaters and generally evil in nature, Schaller's groundbreaking study provided momentum that the conservation movement in Asia had never had before. The deep concern expressed by political leaders such as Indira Gandhi and Rajiv Gandhi about the fate of the tiger made an enormous difference to policy and to its implementation at grassroots level.

With the ban on hunting, the tiger enjoyed some kind of protection for the first time in centuries. By 1980, a small national park called Ranthambhore, in the state of Rajasthan in north-western India, became a tiger haven, and over the next decade it and places like it reshaped the natural history of the tiger, thanks to the lack of human disturbance. In the 1980s, there were no hunters or people cutting wood and grass in Ranthambhore. Cubs born in these circumstances grew up free of the fear of people and produced cubs that were similarly unconcerned about human observers. It was one of the best periods in our history to watch tigers in the wild—a time that may never come again.

Ranthambhore National Park covers an area of 400 sq km, and at its core are a medieval fort, a rest house known as Jogi Mahal, and three lakes, Padam Talao, Rajbagh, and the seasonal Malik Talao, around which much tiger activity is centred. Ranthambhore's forests are situated at the meeting point of two

A typical scene of Ranthambhore wild tigers, even today.

hill ranges, the Aravallis and the Vindhyas, at the extreme western end of the tiger's Indian territory.

What follows is the story of the life of the tiger as I was able to observe it in Ranthambhore in the 1980s and early 1990s, with examples and additional information from scientists and conservationists around the world. Many secrets revealed during this time about the life of the tiger helped to combat the idea of the tiger being the most fearful and dreaded beast of the jungle.

Birth

Gestation varies from 93 to 110 days, with records of captive tigers indicating that 103 days (about three and a half months) is the norm. Cubs may be born at any time of the year—there seems to be no significant seasonal variation, even in harsh climates such as Siberia.

It is difficult to spot a pregnant tigress in the wild, as the bulge of her belly is visible only during the last ten to twelve days of pregnancy. However, she is heavy and may struggle to find sufficient food as hunting becomes more difficult. In his book *Tiger Trails in Assam* (1961), a tea planter named Patrick Hanley describes finding a heavily pregnant tigress lying in tall elephant grass at the edge of a tea estate. For two weeks, a male tiger brought her portions of kills, and when he arrived he would call out to her with a strange cry as if asking her to come out and start eating. This was an unusual incident—for the most part, the expectant mother is on her own.

In the last ten to fifteen days of her pregnancy, a tigress tends to become preoccupied with finding a safe place in which to give birth. This may be in a cave, under a rock overhang, or within a patch of thick bush

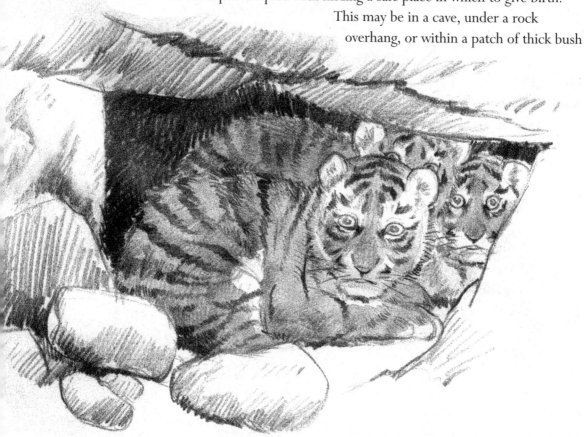

Tiny cubs not even a few weeks old, cuddled up in their den. At this stage of their growth, they are especially vulnerable and totally dependent on their mother.

with dense cover all around. As the time of delivery approaches, she will spend most of her time in the vicinity of the den, familiarizing herself with every corner of the terrain, including details of water supply and the movements of other animals. Her chosen spot not only must have sufficient prey within easy striking range but also must be able to conceal her cubs from predators on the ground and in the sky.

Zoo records indicate that a litter of cubs can be born within one hour, but sometimes the birth takes as long as twenty-four hours, during which time the tigress gets some nourishment from eating the placentas and embryonic sacs. The cubs are born blind and helpless, weighing between 785 and 1610 gm. It takes anywhere from three to fourteen days for their eyes to open, though full vision is not acquired until some weeks later. There may be as many as six or seven cubs in a litter, though in Ranthambhore the norm is three. The average recorded in zoos and in Chitwan National Park in Nepal is just under three, and in the harsher conditions of the Russian Far East it is between 1.2 and 1.9. The ratio of the sexes at birth is one to one. The tigress now becomes a committed, caring, and ruthlessly protective mother.

The First Months

The youngest cubs I have seen in Ranthambhore were about ten weeks old. This was in March 2002, when Mike Birkhead, a film producer with whom I was associated, and I found four cubs with their mother and were able to watch and film them for long periods. Surprisingly, the tigress was walking her little cubs down the middle of a road and seemed perfectly comfortable in the presence of human observers. Tiger mothers are very individualistic in their behaviour when they have cubs. But whether they are shy and elusive or relaxed and confident, finding sufficient food is vital, as the tigress must keep herself well fed in order to provide enough milk to nourish her family.

These early hunting forays must be nerve-racking times for the tigress, with half her mind always on the safety of her cubs. If disturbed, she will be aggressive and may even charge to kill, whether the disturbance comes from other predators, scavengers, or human intruders. I know of three occasions in the last five years when a patrolling party in Ranthambhore has had a fleeting glimpse of a tigress with tiny cubs tucked away in thick bush surrounded by high grass. In each case, they were charged by the furious mother and escaped by the skin of their teeth.

A tigress treats any intrusion into the area where she has hidden her cubs with great suspicion, and if sufficiently disturbed she is likely to abandon the den. She moves her helpless cubs one by one, holding each by the scruff of the neck as it hangs from her mouth and whimpers, and leaving it in the safety of the new den before returning for the next cub. I have witnessed such a scene, and it is amazing to see this supreme predator holding her cubs so gently with those fearsome teeth. A solo parent, the tigress is alone in providing this protection and security, doing the job efficiently and with great care.

Tiger cubs are vulnerable in their first few months, with mortality as high as 50 per cent, sometimes more. They may fall victim to attacks by wild dogs, leopards, snakes, or other tigers, so all their mother's attention goes into keeping them alive and healthy. She spends endless time licking and cleaning them to promote better circulation and bowel movements. She also eats their faeces, which may make it more difficult for potential predators to pick up their smell.

In the first month, the intensely protective mother might change dens if she feels threatened or disturbed. Here, a tigress is shown gently carrying her cub to a new den.

As the days roll by and the cubs grow, they become frisky, starting limited exploratory ventures around their den and playing with leaves, branches, and anything else that takes their fancy. By the time they are six to eight weeks old, their mother is carrying meat back to the den for them, and I once followed the drag marks of a chital (the Indian spotted deer, and along with the sambar deer—the largest deer in India, standing 5 feet at the shoulders and weighing 320 kg or more—a favourite prey of tigers in Ranthambhore) nearly 1.5 km from where it was killed before I lost it in a thick gorge. Unlike a lioness, a tigress will open up a kill for her cubs, but she rarely eats first unless her cubs are very young.

Family Life

In March 1985, after nine years of watching tigers, I had my first real insight into family life when I discovered a tigress named Laxmi with a brood of three small cubs. On the day I encountered her, I was driving in my jeep. In the distance, two sambar hinds moved gingerly away, tails half raised. A chital, motionless, looked sharply toward the forest. I was unable to pick out anything. The shrill alarm of a peacock broke the silence, then another peacock picked up the call. After a few seconds, the alarm call of the chital pierced my ears. Frenzied and frequent calling surrounded me. Quietly, I watched the forest. It sounded as if the tigers must be walking toward the vehicle track.

Suddenly, shades of tan and black emerged from the dull yellow of the forest. Laxmi appeared with three tiny cubs, one of which jumped across the road. It looked about two and a half to three months old. It was my first glimpse ever of cubs this size. Laxmi settled down on

Cubs are suckled by their mother for several months. These four-month-olds subsist on a diet of both milk and meat.

the track for a few minutes. Her cubs looked at me furtively from the cover of a bush. She soon rose and paced leisurely into the forest, followed by the three scampering cubs. They moved toward a network of ravines and disappeared from sight. I rushed back to base, my heart pounding with excitement.

The next morning, I found Laxmi sitting in a patch of grass 10–15 m from the forest track. Her three cubs surrounded her. One nuzzled her face, another rested against her back, the third watched us curiously,

TIGERS IN THE WILD
A.A. Dunbar Brander

Before the cubs are born, the sexes separate, the tigress preferring to be alone until the cubs have a sense of the fitness of things, and the correct attitude towards their male parent. I have known two instances in which a young male tiger had apparently annoyed his father over the dead buffalo they were eating, and in consequence was killed and partly devoured. I came on another case in which a young tiger had been killed and eaten, in which there was no 'bone of contention'.

—*Wild Animals in Central India*, London: Edward Arnold, 1923 moving tentatively toward us before rushing back to the security of its mother. The cubs turned their attention on one another, leaping into the air and knocking into one another. Then they dashed toward Laxmi. She licked one of them thoroughly, then lay down on her side to suckle them. All three soon found a teat and fed, stimulating the flow of milk with their tiny paws. For fifteen minutes I watched this remarkable spectacle. I have never seen such a display of love and warmth, such evidence of the strong bond between a tigress and her cubs.

All this activity seems to continue without the presence of a father, as the male is said to leave the female immediately after mating. Most of the time while her cubs are young, the tigress must protect them from adult males. Infanticide is common when a new male takes over a territory, and as long ago as 1892 a forest officer named J. Inglis reported in the *Journal of the Bombay Natural History Society* an instance of a mauled cub being found at the site of a fight between a male and female.

However, Sainthill Eardley-Wilmot, also a forest officer, took another view in his book *Forest Life and Sport in India* (1910): 'The male tiger does not seem to be addicted to infanticide, though when they are in confinement this crime is reported as not uncommon: in fact I have seen him in company with cubs of all ages and it is probably the difficulty of finding food for many voracious mouths that ultimately enforces separation.' Eardley-Wilmot's view was not widely accepted—for three quarters of a century after his book was published almost everyone believed that adult male tigers killed cubs. But in the spring of 1986 I observed behaviour at a pool of water in Ranthambhore Park that supported Eardley-Wilmot's assertion. At four in the afternoon Kublai (the resident male) ambled toward the pool and slid into the water, hind legs first, soaking himself completely and leaving just his head visible. (Tigers don't like water splashing in their eyes and most of them enter the water backward.)

About twenty minutes later Nalghati (a resident female) followed and they both lazed around in the water. Minutes later her male cub walked quite nonchalantly toward the pool, not a flicker of surprise or fear on his face, circled the two adults, and entered the water near where Kublai was stretched out. Soon, following her brother, a female cub walked to the pool, entering the water to sit on her mother's paw. Nalghati licked her face. One big happy family: Nalghati, Kublai, and two five-month-old cubs were all in close proximity, soaking themselves in this rather small pool of water.

A half hour later the male cub rose, quickly nuzzled Kublai, and left the pool. The female cub followed him and they played, leaping at each other, slowly drifting toward a tree, clambering up the branches under the protective eye of Kublai. At dusk, Kublai heaved himself out of the water and moved toward the cubs. The cubs rushed up to him and he licked one of them.

When I left, Kublai was sitting a metre or so from the two cubs. I had witnessed what must be one of the most closely kept secrets of a tiger's life and now have the first photographic record in the world of a resident male associating with a tigress and her cubs in his range.

That same month, I saw exactly the same thing happening in another part of the forest. Just at the edge of Semli, in the gorge of Bakaula, we found the Bakaula male and Laxmi sitting on the vehicle track facing each other. Thick groves of jamun trees, cool, lush, and green, lined both sides of the track. There were pools of water of various sizes nearby. Laxmi rose briefly and nuzzled the Bakaula male before moving a little way ahead to lie down on her side.

A rare photograph of a tiger family cooling off in a water hole. It is uncommon for a resident male (in front) to be observed with a tigress and her cubs.

The tranquil scene was disturbed by the distant sound of a rolling pebble. Both tigers became alert. Laxmi moved stealthily toward the sound. The Bakaula male sat up expectantly. A sambar walked carefully down an incline. Laxmi was too far away to attack, but the sambar's path was taking it unknowingly toward the Bakaula male, who crouched, muscles tense. The sambar approached the vehicle track. The tiger took  off like a bullet. Six bounds and he leapt onto the back of the sambar, bringing it crashing down. He quickly transferred his grip to the sambar's throat. At the same instant a group of noisy tourists arrived and disturbed the male, who walked off behind a bush, leaving the sambar injured but not quite dead.

Laxmi arrived. Comfortable in the presence of jeeps, she gripped the sambar's throat for a couple of minutes, ensuring that there was no life left in it, and started the tedious process of dragging the 180-kg carcass away, a few metres at a time, into thick cover. The Bakaula male watched her carefully. The carcass was now some 15 m inside the jamun grove, at the edge of a small clearing. The male moved toward it.

An amusing scene now confronted us: the male tiger, with his forepaws on the sambar's rump, had a firm grip on one of the hind legs; Laxmi had a firm grip on the throat. The carcass was stretched between the two tigers. A tug-of-war ensued as each tried to pull the carcass a little toward itself. Both tigers emitted low-pitched growls, interspersed with Herculean tugs at the carcass. Then, with a sudden burst of energy and strength, Laxmi yanked the carcass some 4 m away with the Bakaula male astride its rump: a remarkable feat, as sambar and tiger together must weigh about 450 kg. But the effort exhausted her and she let go of the sambar's throat. The male quickly pulled the carcass out of sight.

Laxmi strode off. Entering a dry streambed that led to her den, she started to call loudly and was greeted by bird-like squeaks from her cubs. In minutes Laxmi returned to the site of the struggle with the cubs running around her in circles. They seemed quite relaxed, as if this wasn't the first occasion on which they were going to share a feast with the Bakaula male. Soon they all disappeared out of sight to where the Bakaula male and the carcass lay. Twice I had seen a remarkable facet of the family life of tigers—the resident male playing the role of father.

Protective Mother

In March 2003, in the Bandhavgarh National Park in central India, a resident male tiger in his prime was frequently found spending time in the company of a tigress and her four seven-month-old cubs. A colleague visited the area at that time and was told that the female, who was suckling her cubs, had even suckled the male.

From these observations it became clear that a resident male fulfilled a paternal role for all the litters in his territory. Contrary to many earlier reports, we saw adult males sharing kills with their cubs, spending time

A tigress in the process of killing a female sambar. The cubs watch their mother very carefully. One of them pats the sambar with its paws. It is a process of learning, and the tigress is an expert teacher.

with them, and protecting the area from other tigers so that the youngsters had a secure environment in which to grow up.

In Ranthambhore, it is rare to hear of a fatal encounter between tigers, especially between a male and a female. If these do occur the natural cycle of a forest destroys the evidence, burying it in the earth. In all the years I have been following tigers, I know of only one example of mortal combat, and it demonstrates how fiercely a tigress will defend her cubs when she encounters a transient male. From traces I discovered the next morning, I was able to reconstruct what must have happened.

There was a full moon on the night of 10 November 1981, when a tigress with two cubs was apparently walking down the Lahpur valley, nearly 20 km from Jogi Mahal, the rest house in the park. She must have spotted an adult male tiger walking in the opposite direction. There were signs that the cubs had scampered away. The tigress seems to have continued toward the tiger, and there were marks where both had sat down in the middle of the road. They must then have risen and gone to sit in the sandy part of a nearby streambed, perhaps an attempt on the part of the tigress to show affection and thus pacify the male and then bid him a rapid farewell before there was any possibility of contact between him and the cubs. Apparently, the cubs attempted to scamper back to their mother, probably finding the insecurity of separation too much to take.

The havoc this caused was heard at a guard post some 2 km away. The male must have moved in a flash toward the cubs, forcing the mother to take lightning action. With a leap and a bound she attacked the male from the rear, clawing his right foreleg before sinking in her canines and killing him. Likely caught completely by surprise, he quickly succumbed. Later, the tigress proceeded to open his rump and eat off his left hind leg. (In this instance, and in most cases of tiger cannibalism, a part of the defeated animal is eaten to prove domination.) This was a rare example of tiger eating tiger and a graphic demonstration of the complete devotion of the mother to the safety of her cubs.

W.D. Ritchie, a British forest officer who stayed in India after Independence, recorded a similar fight in Assam in 1950, when a tigress killed a big male, presumably also to protect her cubs. She, too, ate a chunk of meat from his carcass.

A tigress boxes out at a male to prevent him from appropriating her kill and threatening her cubs.

Family and the Competition for Food

By the time they are six months old, the cubs are weaned and roam around more freely. They are now the size of large dogs, and the tigress moves them greater distances, her hunting range expanding considerably as the youngsters familiarize themselves with various landmarks; observe the habits of prey and the way their mother stalks, kills, and eats it; explore waterholes; and generally learn about the forest. The tigress now has two major concerns: training her cubs to hunt and to fend for themselves, and procuring enough food for them all. The cubs are growing fast, their increased appetites demanding a constant supply of food. They are not mature enough to help their mother hunt; indeed, they are more likely to get in her way and spoil her chances of making a kill. It is during this period that she instils discipline with the occasional slap and sharp growl, and through a complex series of sounds the cubs are trained to avoid danger and to remain quiet when their mother hunts. In fact, on her instruction they can remain rooted to a spot for hours on end.

By the time the cubs are eight to ten months old, mother and youngsters are beginning to hunt together. Hunting is now a full-time obsession—a tigress with two cubs has to kill seventy to seventy-five deer-sized animals in a year, about 45 per cent more than her solo requirement, to ensure that there is enough food to go around.

On a memorable morning in 1987, I was watching Noon, one of the females I was able to study most closely during that time. I had stopped near Rajbagh, but the barking of a langur monkey from the side of the lake spurred me on. The sun was just rising over a hill. Amid a cacophony of chital, sambar, and langur calls, I turned a corner to find Noon walking nonchalantly with a chital fawn swinging in her mouth. As she walked along the shore of the lake, a few peahens took flight. She headed for a bank of high grass, startling two peacocks. The male cub, in the lead, grabbed the fawn from Noon's jaws and darted back to a clump

A tigress carries a small chital back to her cubs: when prey is small it dangles from her mouth as she carries it, the legs of the victim making drag marks on the forest floor. Sometimes drag marks can go on for up to 2 km.

of grass. Noon licked her female cub, and they both reclined at the edge of the grass. The male polished off most of the carcass, but toward the end Noon interrupted him. He snarled at her, but she ignored him and picked up the remnants.

The female joined her mother, and they chewed on the bits and pieces the male had left. An hour went by, and then mother and cubs left the grass, walking along the edge of the lake toward Padam Talao. The cubs jumped and chased each other as they walked around the lake. One charged into Noon, and she snarled in annoyance. All three reached the edge of the first lake. The cubs turned a corner and disappeared.

Noon walked in front of us on the vehicle track. Two sambar alarm calls blasted the silence. The cubs had been seen. Noon was now completely alert and darted forward on the track, realizing that the sambar was caught between the track and her cubs. The cubs assisted her unintentionally. There was a thud of hooves and a noise in the undergrowth. Noon settled down on her belly, frozen to the ground at a point where a narrow animal path led out from the edge of the lake. She judged the exit point exactly. A large rock hid her. In a flash, she leaped into the forest and was out of sight. I heard a grunt.

Driving a little farther, I saw Noon a few metres off the track, in the process of killing a sambar hind. She had a perfect grip on the throat.

The sambar's legs twisted in vain; her hold was firm. The cubs approached cautiously and watched their mother intently. The male cub moved to the carcass, but a flicker from the sambar's hind leg forced it to retreat. In minutes, the sambar was dead. The cub rested his forepaw on the rump, while Noon held her grip and the female cub stood near her mother. Noon dragged the carcass away to where a thick bush made visibility difficult. The cubs jumped all over the sambar and their mother. A kill of this size fed mother and cubs for three days.

One of the largest litters I ever had the privilege of observing numbered five cubs, born to the tigress Padmini in 1977. A litter of this size is rare, the only other example I know of being recorded was by R.C. Morris, forest officer, in 1925.

As the months following my encounter with Padmini and her cubs went by, sightings of the cubs became more frequent, and I found that there were three males and two females. One of the females was in poor condition and lagged behind. She was obviously getting the smallest share of the meat. Padmini's task was enormous: to hunt and kill for such a large brood, now needing at least 20–30 kg of meat per day. By the following month, there was no sign of the small female, and I felt sure that nature must have taken its course. Survival is only of the fittest, and feeding five cubs is no easy task.

Threats to Cubs

Until the age of about fourteen to fifteen months, the cubs spend much of their time playing either with one another or with their mother. Bouts of play can be long and tiring as the cubs charge and swat at one another and even race up and down trees, something they continue to do until they become too heavy—it also provides a haven if they are threatened by wild dogs or other tigers. Adult tigers do not climb trees under normal circumstances, but when cornered by hunters they have been known to take refuge in surprisingly high branches. In the *Journal of the Bombay Natural History Society* in 1923, a government officer named G.E.R. Cooper reported an incident of a tiger climbing 11 m up toward a machan (the raised platform used by tiger hunters).

An eight-month-old cub atop a tree.

During the floods of 1969 in the Sundarbans delta in north-eastern India, tigers climbed up trees 10 m high to escape drowning. But these were exceptional circumstances. In Ranthambhore I have seen tigers on trees about ten times, and only once was it an adult tigress, who was sitting on the lowest branches. On all the other occasions it was cubs, whether in play or to escape from danger.

In 2001–2, a resident tigress named Machli was rearing two male cubs, who spent endless time charging back and forth on the edge of the lake, splashing water at each other and playing hide-and-seek in the tall grass. They would snarl and hiss at sunbathing crocodiles, which would turn on them, sending them scampering back to cover. All these activities strengthen the cubs' muscles and flex their limbs for what lies ahead.

Nevertheless, the mother has to be alert to any kind of danger. In the first few months, the resident male who had fathered Machli's litter kept a protective eye on them, but suddenly he vanished, and within a couple of months younger male tigers were vying for the area and the tigress's attentions. When new males kill cubs it brings the female back into estrus, enabling a newcomer to mate with her and sire cubs of his own. Given the chance, he will kill small cubs of both sexes; however, once they are about a year old he seems to tolerate the females, perhaps viewing them as future reproductive partners, whereas he will kill the males, whom he presumably sees as potential rivals.

Machli had enormous difficulty keeping her cubs safe from the new males. Along with a colleague, I watched her over a two-week period during which she roared constantly, asserting her territorial rights to the area and demonstrating her aggression toward the intruders. She even fought one of them off, clawing his paw and forcing him to limp away. Her whole nature had changed—she was much more watchful and tense, buying time so that the cubs could reach subadulthood unscathed. She even seduced one of the new males, briefly allowing him to mate with her. This was the first time I had noticed something like this, although a similar incident occurred in Panna National Park. These are the only examples I know of a tigress giving

At twelve months old, cubs frequently run, stalk, and leap. The play between cubs will determine their hunting abilities in the future.

temporary 'conjugal rights' to a new male and thereby protecting her cubs from infanticide.

Machli succeeded in raising her cubs and quickly conceived again once they matured and left her to carve out their own territories elsewhere. By this time, her mate had established himself as the new resident of the area, and everything was much calmer. Machli's actions prove that a tigress can protect her cubs till adulthood even when the male who fathered the litter is gone, though only with difficulty.

Avoiding danger may be even more challenging when the threat comes from humans. In September 2002, as part of an organized protest, hundreds of people armed with long sticks, muzzle-loading guns, and swords led thousands of head of livestock into Ranthambhore National Park to graze illegally. The place where they camped was the heart of the territory of a superb tigress who had four nine-month-old cubs. It was a traumatic day. No one now knows exactly what happened, but the tigress was probably poisoned along with two of her cubs. The other two survived and were found roaming a patch of forest in a starved condition. In the absence of their mother, cubs of that age normally die, since they have no idea how to hunt. In addition, the monsoon of 2002 was virtually non-existent, so Ranthambhore was in the grip of the severest drought in decades. In an attempt to keep the cubs alive and see whether they could learn to fend for themselves, the park authorities fed these two orphaned cubs goats, but the cubs had a tough year ahead of them nonetheless. In March 2003 they were both alive, their permanent teeth had replaced their milk teeth—a key factor in a young tiger's ability to fend for itself—and the male cub was able to kill small chital. The female still needed goats. She had also started to focus her attention on the fringe of the forest in her search for food, where there was a danger that she would start taking livestock and come into conflict with the forest communities. When this happens, local grazers may deliberately poison carcasses in revenge. Monitoring the female became essential. The incident was a tragic example of how easy it is for people to destroy an entire tiger family.

Learning Adult Skills

It is the mother's skill in training her cubs
that ensures their survival. Until the age of
eighteen months, cubs are dependent on
their mother's hunting abilities. Our
observations of Padmini's large litter made
clear the trouble a tigress takes to show her
offspring how to hunt for themselves.

Padmini spent a lot of time trying to
prevent us from seeing her cubs. In fact,
twice she led us off in pursuit, allowing
the cubs to evade us. Nevertheless, I had a marvellous opportunity to
observe the growing-up process. The cub known as Akbar was the
most confident of the four and always came closest to us, followed by
Babar and Hamir, and finally the only female, Laxmi.

Late one evening, I spotted the family by the side of a road. Akbar
was sitting boldly in front, with Padmini and Laxmi sleeping behind
him. Our presence heralded some interaction, with Laxmi getting up
and nuzzling her mother, and Padmini returning her gesture with a few
licks. Babar and Hamir played in the distance, circling each other and
mock pawing. Akbar rose suddenly and, in a few bounds, leaped
toward his brothers. Hamir rose in anticipation and they greeted each
other—both rising on their hind feet and boxing each other gently with
their forepaws.

We wanted to observe the behaviour of the family around a kill. The
park director brought a buffalo and turned it loose close by the tigers.
Padmini moved in a flash, but instead of killing it she chose to
incapacitate it with a blow to its hindquarters. She then withdrew and
sat a little distance away. The injured buffalo limped around in front of
the cubs. Very cautiously, Akbar and Hamir approached it, but the
buffalo charged them clumsily, and they rushed away into high grass.
Again they emerged, with Babar and Laxmi following, taking up four
positions to encircle the prey, but whenever they tried to go in close the

buffalo charged. This little scene lasted thirty minutes while Padmini looked on. Suddenly, Akbar leaped toward the buffalo, landing on its hindquarters and bringing it down. After several clumsy movements he sank his canines into the animal's neck. Hamir now entered the fray and sat on the rump. Soon they started eating, but after some twenty minutes Padmini rose and moved them off, walking toward Babar and Laxmi and nudging them as if to say, 'Come on, it's your turn.' Being shyer than their brothers, they did not get up and feed until Akbar and Hamir had eaten their fill. Padmini then started feeding herself. She was not only allowing the cubs to learn how to kill but also ensuring the equal sharing of food.

This method of training the young has been recorded by many observers, among them forest officer Frederick C. Hicks, who wrote in *Forty Years among the Wild Animals of India* (1910): 'If cubs are present, the hind leg of the kill will frequently be found to be broken, the idea being to disable the animal and then to play with it alive for the edification of the cubs, while the nose, ears, and eyes will invariably be found much gnawed and torn by the cubs.' George Schaller witnessed a tigress teaching her three-year-old cubs to kill a tethered buffalo, which kept them at bay for two and a half hours—the tigress twice had to throw the prey to the ground to assist the cubs' endeavours.

Until the cubs are about fourteen or fifteen months, the tigress tends, in my experience, to give way to them on a kill, allowing them to eat first, but in the last months that the cubs are with her she becomes much more aggressive and will eat first if she chooses. As the cubs grow, they actively assist their mother in the hunt, even though they are still clumsy and sometimes get in the way.

The strong bonds that persist between members of a tiger family are remarkable. Some ten years after the incident described above, I was watching Laxmi, now with three cubs of her own, two females and a male. One warm afternoon in March 1987, I arrived at a water hole to find Laxmi's cubs resting in the cool of the undergrowth. One of the females moved toward us, in her normal way, walking very close to the jeep. There was no sign of Laxmi. The cubs lazed around for nearly an hour, but at four o'clock one of them suddenly became alert. It darted off to the far side of the water hole, followed by its siblings. The forest exploded with the sound of purring as the cubs exhaled great bursts of what sounded like joy. I followed to find the cubs rubbing their flanks against Laxmi. All four tigers purred incessantly, as if orchestrated, as the cubs licked, nuzzled, and cuddled their mother. The sounds echoed and resounded with great intensity. Although they are capable of a wide range of sounds, tigers are basically silent animals, and vocalization is rare. In all my years of tiger watching in Ranthambhore I have never heard purring the way I did on this occasion.

The purring continued for nearly ten minutes, as all four tigers walked toward us. The cubs rubbed their bodies against Laxmi, expressing their delight at seeing her. They moved to the water hole and quenched their thirst, then Laxmi moved some 20 m away to rest in the shade of a tree. The cubs returned to their original positions.

It was nearly five when I decided to watch from a distance, hoping that some deer would come to the water hole to quench their thirst. At six o'clock, a group of fourteen chital emerged from the cover of the forest

Stalking its prey step by step, as if in slow motion.

and cautiously approached the water. Laxmi was suddenly alert, watching intensely. The deer had not seen her or the cubs. The cubs froze, knowing that the slightest movement would give them away. Most of the deer had their tails up, a sign that they at least sensed the tigers' presence. They stood between the mother and her cubs, a perfect situation for Laxmi. She crouched, then moved forward some 3 m on her belly as if gliding along the ground. A chital alarm call pierced the evening.

Laxmi moved in a flash. Her cubs sprinted from the far side, and in the panic and confusion of the moment a fawn became separated from the group and fled toward the tigress, who pinioned it between her paws and grabbed the back of its neck. The fawn squealed and died. A stork-billed kingfisher flew away from its perch, its blue wings glinting in the evening light. Picking up the fawn, Laxmi carried it away.

Her cubs moved in, hoping to feast on a few morsels. Laxmi dropped the fawn to the ground and settled on it, covering the tiny carcass with her paws. She turned and snarled viciously at the approaching cubs. One of the females moved off, but the other two settled down a metre away to face their mother. Both emitted low-pitched moaning sounds, which I had never heard before. The noises soon turned into wails, as if the cubs were begging for the carcass. Laxmi snarled and coughed sharply at

Two young cubs laze around at the spot where their mother has left them. She is able to instil such discipline in them that the cubs will not move an inch till she returns.

them. The male cub rose and moved toward her, but she growled, picking up the carcass and lying down again some 3 m away, the fawn between her paws.

All three cubs now settled around her, moaning. She snarled in response, and this continued for fifteen minutes. Suddenly, two of the cubs cannonballed into her, and all three tigers rolled over in a flurry of activity; then the male cub snatched the carcass expertly and rushed away with it, followed by one of his sisters. Laxmi sat unconcerned and began to groom herself. The male would not tolerate his sisters on the carcass, so they returned to their mother. They watched their brother eating, waiting patiently for forty-five minutes until the fawn had been consumed. Then they all moved on. When the prey is tiny, the dominant cub asserts his right to eat most of it. He shares only when the kill is large.

The Break-up of the Family

By the age of sixteen months, young tigers have grown the permanent teeth that enable them to kill prey effectively. At this time, the hierarchical order among cubs becomes clearly defined: the dominant one has the pick of everything and will always eat first. Although this is most frequently a male, I have seen two litters in which the dominant cub was a female who totally tyrannized her brother. Whatever its sex, the dominant cub is now more confident, aggressive, and even able to push its mother around. Eating on a carcass may follow a strict 'pecking order', and if the cubs are three or four in number and the prey small, the least dominant one rarely gets a chance to eat.

Within a few months, the dominant cub will leave the family unit, followed in due course by his or her siblings. Up to the age of twenty-two months and sometimes even later, subadults will still join their mother on kills, even though they are spending most of the rest of the time away from her. In this way, they are assured of a supply of food while they continue to polish their own hunting skills.

In 2003, when Machli's two male cubs were nearly eighteen months old and ready to leave her, I witnessed an encounter that revealed the intense bonds that exist between mother and cubs, even at this age. Although both cubs were now the same size as their mother, she nevertheless allowed them to suckle for ten minutes. Not that she had any milk—it was more like a farewell gesture, with the young tigers experiencing a mother's ultimate connection with her child for the last time.

I often wonder what exactly happens as family groups break up. After watching wild tigers for decades, I remain convinced that you cannot generalize about this or anything else to do with their behaviour. At the same time as Machli's eighteen-month-old cubs were leaving her to lead their own lives, the Lahpur family in another part of the park was still together, though the youngsters were twenty-four months old. In fact, the two male cubs tended to roam around together while the female and her mother kept together, and they would all meet up to feed on a kill, irrespective of who had made it. I had an amazing opportunity to witness this in January 2003, when the Lahpur female killed an enormous sambar stag and all four tigers gathered around the kill. Feeding was controlled by the mother, amid a diversity of snarling, growling, low-pitched sounds, and much submission among the cubs. The young female inched her way forward to partake in the feast and succeeded. This was in itself an amazing sight, as she squirmed and squeezed her way in, forcing her two big brothers to give way. The next morning, the mother was gone, but all three cubs—subadults, really— were chewing at the bones. Because they had eaten they were much more relaxed than they had been the evening before.

So, family links and associations, especially over food, can continue even after the age of two years. In April 2003, when the Lahpur cubs were nearly twenty-seven months, the two brothers were still hunting together and feeding on the same kills. I saw both of them just after the smaller male had killed a female nilgai. I watched him as he squatted right on top of the carcass, telling the world that he owned it. Then he slipped away. Late in the evening, I had a glimpse of both brothers. Throughout the day they had not eaten a morsel—perhaps they were too nervous in our presence. When I returned the next morning, I saw them both in the distance. Somehow, they had managed to drag a 200-kg antelope at least 400 m away so that they could eat in private.

Range, Territory, and Mobility

Usually, when tigers reach the age of eighteen to twenty-four months, their mother, ready to mate again, forces them out of the family unit. In Ranthambhore, males tend to spend their first independent years around the fringes of the forest, transecting the ranges of one or more dominant males. Sometimes brothers will remain together for a few months. But this movement outward is temporary; in a year or two, they will move back into the heart of the forest, ready to usurp the resident males, take control of important hunting grounds, and mate with the females who live there. This continuous process of assertion results in much shifting and adjusting. Levels of mortality can be very high—as much as 35 per cent—as the young males come into conflict with territory holders and have to fight to establish themselves. Until that happens, they are like drifters looking for a bed each night. They may continue to float around in this way till they are four to four and a half years old, struggling to keep alive but at the same time maturing and building up their strength.

A tiger exploring the forest in search of a new range to live in.

Two tigers explore the receding waters of a water hole before the beginning of the monsoon.

It is believed that tigers can walk up to 30 km in one night. During its period of transition, a young male may range over an area of up to 200 sq km.

A female of twenty-four to thirty-six months has a much easier time of it than her brothers—her cohort's mortality rate is only about 5 per cent. She tends to remain in her mother's range, which slowly shrinks to accommodate her. I know that this happened with Machli and one of her daughters, Broken Tail, who stayed very close to the area where she was born and whose range overlapped with that of her mother. It is not unusual to find a number of adjacent areas serving as homes to related tigresses, with a lot of overlap. My experience reveals that overlap is not altogether uncommon with males, too.

Those who study tigers are keenly interested in the size of a tiger's range or territory. (These terms are used fairly loosely: the area where a female lives is usually described as her home range, while a male patrols a larger area generally called a territory, which many encompass the range of as many as five or, as in one exceptional case in Nepal, seven females.) It seems that the presence of females, rather than availability of prey, is what makes a territory attractive to a male, whereas a female, probably instinctively aware that she will have cubs to rear, is more

interested in resources. So when a male takes over a territory, he is likely
to acquire both females and resources. In Ranthambhore, a male's
territory may vary from 5 to 150 sq km, while in Panna one is known to
have covered 280 sq km and included the range of three females. In the
icy cold of Siberia, where prey populations are much less concentrated,
males can have territories of 800 to 1200 sq km. By contrast, females in
Ranthambhore have occupied 5 to 25 sq km, in Panna 30 to 50 sq km,
and in the Russian Far East 200 to 500 sq km. In other words, there is
tremendous variation from place to place.

To a large extent, the size of a territory depends on the density of
prey and can vary seasonally because of monsoon, drought, or any other
event that affects the availability of food. At one time, twelve tigers
shared the area around the lakes in Ranthambhore. At another time,
there was only one. So there have been tremendous fluctuations even in
the same place. But at any given moment one tiger or tigress reigns
supreme in any one spot, and no other is tolerated. If another appears,

A tiger cools off.

one or the other will submit by rolling on its back, or else there will be a fierce fight.

In Chitwan National Park it has been established that females move on average 9.7 km from their natal range, while males move 33 km. In Ranthambhore, males move fewer than 15 km, but this may be because Ranthambhore is an 'island' of forest surrounded by a large area that is inhospitable to tigers. Under these circumstances, there is likely to be even more conflict than usual between males, and a lot of youngsters probably perish because there is nowhere for them to go. A large area of connected habitat is vital if subadults are going to disperse evenly and survive. Some scientists working in areas that have healthy densities of tigers consider that most dispersing cubs could end up as part of a 'doomed surplus' that has little chance of finding a range or territory in which to function. These young floaters are bound to perish as forest areas become more and more fragmented.

What is particularly interesting is the number of changes and shifts that occur during the monsoon. Soon afterward, during October, when it is possible to go out looking for tigers after a lull of several weeks, I often find that new animals have arrived.

Until October 1982, the area around the three lakes in Ranthambhore was occupied by two transient males, one of whom was probably Genghis, who became the dominant male and was one of the most remarkable tigers I have ever watched. There were also Padmini and her three nearly adult cubs; and two other females, Nick Ear, who was Padmini's daughter from a previous litter, and Nasty, so named because of her aggressive nature. She was quite the fiercest tigress I have encountered in my years of tiger watching.

Padmini's daughter Laxmi, then about five years old, was also occasionally seen at the edges of the third lake with three cubs of her own. These tigresses' ranges overlapped for several months, but by the end of 1982 there were few signs of Padmini and her latest family, except for one memorable occasion described later. She shifted her range to the far side of the forest, leaving her former range completely and never returning. Her cubs survived to maturity, but I lost track of them after they separated from their mother.

So at this time some twelve tigers of varying ages lived in the limited area of the 3–4 sq km around the lakes. For a year after Padmini moved away, most of our sightings were of Nick Ear, one other female, and the two males. I saw very little of Nasty after the middle of 1983, but Nick Ear could be found around the lakes nearly every day. Then, for no apparent reason, she, too, disappeared.

By October 1984, Genghis had moved out, and the area was frequented by another large male, named Kublai. Initially very elusive, he slowly became more confident, spending a lot of time marking and asserting his presence. He was totally different from Genghis in his general behaviour, though he used the same paths, niches, and water holes. I kept a detailed record through March and April 1985, and from March 16 to April 15 Kublai's pugmarks were always somewhere in the vicinity of the lakes.

These movements and appearances and disappearances are extremely complex, and the reasons underlying them are often far from clear. I know of one instance when a female, wounded in a clash with another tiger, moved 12 km away from her home range to a completely new area. But why did Nick Ear leave when Genghis arrived? Why did Genghis disappear when Kublai arrived? Did Kublai kill Genghis? Or were poachers active? These remain difficult questions, apparently without answers.

Tigers in the Sundarbans can swim large distances across the waterways of the mangrove swamps.

The lakes support large concentrations of deer and are therefore prime hunting grounds for the tiger. This may also be a factor in the changes that occur every year as new tigers take over from old ones—there are always going to be newcomers competing for control in the most desirable areas.

I believe that very seldom do male tigers have non-aggressive contact with other males in their area. As with so many aspects of their behaviour, tigers seem very individualistic in their attitudes toward range and territory and especially toward the sharing of it. In 1923, A.A. Dunbar Brander, a forest officer working in India, observed three adult males hunting together, and both George Schaller and Billy Arjan Singh have recorded cordial associations between resident and transient male tigers. I have only once seen two adult males

strolling together and then stalking off in search of prey. I have also
seen two male siblings clash just after breaking away from the family,
but before things could become vicious one of the males submitted,
rolling on his back twice, and peace descended. Males in a given area
probably establish a rank order, which is then accepted by all, though I
know that Genghis never tolerated another male in the area for the
year that he ruled the Ranthambhore lakes. When territorial conflict
does take place, evidence suggests that it is ferocious and blood-
curdling, and Ranthambhore must have seen huge battles between
male tigers, but I have never observed them with my own eyes, nor do
I know anyone who has.

Mobility among tigers is an ever-changing phenomenon, affected by
seasonal variations, prey movement, and the availability of water. Tigers

seem to move around more in the winter than in the intense summer heat, probably because of the cooler temperatures and plentiful water, a process that disperses the prey species otherwise found around the numerous water holes. Tigers are powerful swimmers and can cross lakes and rivers with ease—water seems to be no obstacle to them. Their ranges can encompass lakes and small islands, as in the mangrove swamps of the Sundarbans. According to some observers, the tiger can swim more than 15 km—a truly amazing feat if it is true. A government officer named R.K.M. Battye described the tiger's swimming ability in the *Journal of the Bombay Natural History Society* in 1942:

During several years of shooting in the Sunderbunds [sic] forests, I discovered that tigers readily take to water, and in some instances swim considerable distances (three or four miles), and in a tidal river with a four to five knot tide running during spring tides, but what struck me most, however, was the intelligence displayed by tigers in choosing their time for swimming, which was invariably at or about high water, when they were able to 'take off' and land on hard ground, and anyone who has had experience in the Sunderbunds will appreciate what this means!—At all other states of the tide one has to flounder up several yards of bank through more than knee-deep mud, which would prove very embarrassing to a heavy animal like a tiger.

On 2 March 1858, the crew of the steamer *Aden* killed a tiger that was swimming roughly 11 km from Mumbai. Tigers have been spotted 8 km out to sea near the islands around Singapore and were once known to swim between the islands of Java and Bali—for some of them, the Selat Bali Strait, which is 4 km wide at its narrowest point, must simply have run through part of their territory.

The dense mangrove swamps of the Sundarbans have produced some of the most unusual tiger behaviour ever recorded. M. Monirul H. Khan, a wildlife biologist, explores how these tigers cope with vast waterways, and how their interaction with humans has evolved.

MYSTERIOUS TIGERS OF THE SUNDARBANS
M. Monirul H. Khan

Out of fear and respect people call them *Mama* (uncle). Both Muslims and Hindus worship them. They are rarely seen, but they kill many people every year. They are the mysterious tigers of the Sundarbans— the least known to scientists of all the world's tigers, the only ones that live in mangroves, and yet one of the most thriving populations. The Sundarbans are the largest single mass of tidal mangrove forest on Earth, covering an area of about 10,000 sq. km in the Ganges-Brahmaputra delta of Bangladesh and India. Roughly 60 per cent of this forest is in Bangladesh and the rest in India. Here, the tiger is the flagship species and supreme predator.

Mangroves are very different from other tiger habitats. With the rapid decline of the evergreen and deciduous forests in the north, east, and west of the area—and the subsequent diminution of the prey population—tigers find the Sundarbans a relatively safe but challenging place to colonize. They have to adapt to the semi-aquatic ecosystem, facing a lot of water and mud, and thus they need to swim much more than any other tiger population. This scarcity of land might explain why the Sundarban tigers are thinner than other populations of the same subspecies.

The tiger is classified by the World Conservation Union (IUCN) as a globally endangered species, but its conservation status in Bangladesh is even more dire: there, it is identified as critically endangered. Based on recent pugmark censuses, the tiger population has been estimated to be 362 in the Bangladesh Sundarbans and 263 in the Indian Sundarbans— a total of 625 tigers.

However, the exact number is not very important, so long as there is a sufficiently large and viable population. The population trend is rather more important, and this can be easily monitored from tiger signs. Despite all the deadly conflicts with people, it is still relatively stable, thanks to the natural inaccessibility of the habitat and human fear of man-eating tigers. Since the ecosystem is tidal, the land is suitable neither for agriculture nor for human settlement: this is the main reason why such a huge forest remains intact in one of the most densely populated areas in the world. Perhaps the tiger population in the Sundarbans is one of the largest unfragmented populations on Earth. For these reasons, the area offers vital potential for long-term conservation.

Unlike other tigers, those in the Sundarbans have a reputation for eating people. Officially, tigers killed a total of 173 humans (17.3 per year) in the Bangladesh Sundarbans between 1993 and 2002. During the same period, humans killed thirty tigers (three per year). However, based on field survey it was found that, between September 2001 and February 2003, a total of forty-one humans were killed by tigers while seven tigers were killed by humans. However, the number of humans killed each year is very low in relation to the number working in the Sundarbans (possibly less than 0.05 per cent).

In other tiger ranges, man-eating tigers are rare and are usually either old or injured tigers; in the Sundarbans, however, both healthy and unhealthy tigers were found to become man-eaters with theories about why this should be so ranging from the salinity of the water to easy availability of human prey. In the absence of concrete evidence to prove any theory, however, it might be better to conclude that the man-eating habit is simply a behavioural character of some tigers in the Sundarbans.

The growing concern for tiger conservation among government bodies, international organizations, and people in general is affirmative progress on the road to ensuring that the tiger survives. This magnificent creature has lived in the incredible wilderness of the Sundarbans for hundreds of years, intimately intertwined with the history and culture of the region; hence, the tiger is the national animal of both Bangladesh and India. It is the heart of the Sundarbans. As Asir Johnsingh said, 'Saving the tiger is a challenge for mankind.' We do need to take it as a challenge. We cannot let the tiger become extinct.

M. Monirul H. Khan is a wildlife biologist working on the tiger and other wild animals of Bangladesh. He conducted his PhD fieldwork on the ecology and conservation of the tiger in the Sundarbans of Bangladesh. He has written fifteen scientific articles and many popular articles.

Communication, Marking, and Messages

Not very vocal by nature, tigers use sound far less frequently than, for example, lions. Whenever I hear the roar of a tiger, I feel a surge of excitement and anticipation, because they never vocalize without a specific reason.

The roar is a resonant sound like 'aaoom', which reverberates through the forest and is used by a male to assert his territorial right, either by inviting another tiger to possible conflict or by encouraging his hurried departure. While he was in residence around the Ranthambhore lakes, Genghis spent many evenings roaring and was once heard to roar thirty-six times in eighty-four minutes. I know that on three of these occasions there was a tigress in close proximity, and once he repeatedly answered the roar of another tiger a couple of kilometres away.

Twice I have heard a female and on several occasions a male roaring in response to a cacophony of alarm calls from sambar, chital, and langur monkeys that had spotted the threat of the tiger's presence. The tiger roared as if in annoyance—presumably its chances of hunting successfully were ruined—and most of the alarms fell silent.

Frederick W. Champion captures some of the power of this sound in his book *With a Camera in Tiger-land* (1927):

I remember an occasion when I was waiting ... in a dense jungle just as night was closing in, listening to a roaring tiger coming closer and closer. When it was practically dark the animal came to within twenty yards of where I was waiting, by which time the volume and malignity of the roaring seemed simply appalling. The whole dark forest seemed to vibrate with the very sound and I confess that, accustomed as I am to the roaring of tigers, I began to feel somewhat nervous.

I have heard a tigress moan on several occasions. It is a subdued sound, at a lower pitch than a roar, and is used with great frequency by a female in estrus. The sharp aggressive woof and cough of tigers I have heard only twice. The first time, two males confronted each other in the forest, woofing and leaping and then woofing and coughing, face-to-face at a distance of a few centimetres. It is a very sharp, loud sound, chilling for the listener. On the second occasion, two adult females used much the same sound as they settled to feed on a chital. It is very rare for tigers to feed together, and I imagine that these two were related. As they ate, they also snarled, growled, and hissed. The sounds started off with great ferocity, but after an hour they seemed to fade into a lower key. Champion describes a similar situation: 'For the next hour they quarrelled violently over their meal, making the most awful growls and snarls as they demolished the carcass, while I, shaking with suppressed excitement, sat pondering upon my foolishness in having allowed my machan to be tied in such an insecure position. Every now and then there would be a terrific outburst of snarling as one of them drove the other away from the kill.'

I have heard growling and snarling several times. A tigress annoyed at her subadult cubs emits a low growl that seems to come from deep within her and lingers in the air. Angry tigers mock-charging my jeep make a sharp, aggressive growl-cum-roar as they leap toward me. I have also often been snarled at by tigers I am observing. In this instance, the tiger holds its mouth slightly open, bares its canines, wrinkles its nose, and exhales. I once heard a male who had seized a tigress's kill utter a low, growling snarl whenever she tried to join him; over the space of a couple of hours he drove her farther and farther away. Twice I have heard a strange blowing sound like a continuous puffing, made by a tiger who had settled down to eat after protecting a kill for several hours. Prusten, a puffing sound made by air being pushed out through the nostrils and mouth and audible only at close range, is a part of greeting behaviour.

Young cubs squeak like birds to attract their mother, and, although I have never heard it, there are reports of a 'pooking' that seems to prevent sudden encounters. Purring, grunting, squeaking, and a low rolling growl all add to the tiger's diverse repertoire. R.C. Morris described the sounds of the tiger in the *Journal of the Bombay Natural History Society* of 1953: 'The sound commenced every time with a perfect imitation of a locomotive suddenly letting off steam, lasting only about four or five seconds, followed by a series of guttural "chuckles" repeated from sixty to eighty times; not unlike the chuckles emitted by a hyena. At night this sounds extremely eerie.'

My most exciting week of tiger sound was with Machli in March 2002. During this week, she roared 226 times in my presence—an extraordinary performance for a normally silent cat. At the time, she had

At eighteen months the cubs start marking trees and bushes with their scent. Here two cubs mark the tree, while the third sniffs at the bark.

two cubs aged six or seven months, and she was probably roaring to ensure that a new male tiger kept his distance.

The tiger's ear is many times more sensitive than the human's to both high and low frequencies. On many occasions, tigers have heard animals or humans before I did, although I was watching from only a few feet away. Their ability to pick up high-frequency sound enables them to detect the movements of prey species—the distant thud of a hoof is registered as the ears twitch from side to side, assessing sound much like a rotating radar antenna. Even when the tiger is asleep the ears are continuously receiving sound—as we shall see later in this chapter, this sensitivity is vital to hunting success.

When tigers are able to see one another they communicate through their facial expressions. They use their eyes, the position of their ears, a flick of their tail, and the stretching of their cheeks to express their feelings, whether aggression or affection. The way a tiger moves also reveals its mood.

But more significantly, tigers have devised a way of communicating their movements and establishing their territorial claims through the use of scent. The most important facet of this is spray marking. As an adult tiger of either sex walks along, it will turn its hindquarters toward a tree, bush, or patch of grass, and with tail raised vertically shoot out a spray of fluid, hitting the target at an upward angle. A male's fluid stream is narrow compared with that of a female, but in both sexes the fluid—a mixture of urine and a secretion from the anal glands—smells musky and strong. The smell can last for up to forty days and is an excellent indication of how recently a tiger has passed by and whether or not the area is occupied. This may discourage or encourage other tigers, depending on the situation. Even human observers can identify the spray of an individual tiger if they know its 'marking trees'.

After ejecting this spray, a tiger will often sniff it and then hang its tongue out with nose wrinkled, a gesture known as flehmen. Flehmen is also used when sniffing another tiger's scent—it conveys a wealth of information, such as the age and sex of the owner and whether or not a female is in estrus. Cubs can follow their mother through her scent, and the scent of a tigress in estrus will pinpoint her location for the resident male.

Most scent marking is done on elevated spots such as leaning trees or rock overhangs that are easily accessible for other tigers and that shelter the scents from the rain. A patrolling tiger will scent mark regularly so that the message remains.

Spraying is not the only means of marking an area with scent. A gland between the toes exudes a scent that enables cubs to follow literally in their mother's footsteps. There are also scent glands in the tail, around the anus, and on the cheeks and chin. Tigers frequently roll

A tiger claws the bark of a tree to leave a territorial signal for other tigers.

In the first few months, tiger cubs are totally dependent on their mother for food and protection.

As they grow up, the cubs play among themselves (top, left), watch their mother hunt (bottom, right), and learn to mark trees (top, right)—all under the watchful eyes of their mother, and in rare instances the father as well (bottom, left).

Hunting is the most vital skill the cubs learn from their mother. A tiger's hunting techniques vary tremendously, depending on the individual and its mood.

The tiger and some of the other creatures that share the same environment. Saving them would help save India's wildlife and our environment.

The many moods
of the tiger.

in patches of grass in order to leave their scents, and they also rub their cheeks on the bark of trees. All the scent glands are at work to communicate a tiger's presence for territorial and reproductive reasons.

Fresh scent can indicate a danger, especially between males, whereas an old scent may be a signal that the animal can go ahead with care. But whether the scent is stale or fresh, a passing tiger will always sniff at it and spray over it, thereby asserting his or her own claim to the spot. I have on several occasions seen a tigress at the edge of her range, sniffing the scent of another and immediately retracing her steps. Scent marking is at its peak on the fringes of territories, where it helps to prevent direct confrontations and avoid conflict.

Up until 1980, I had never seen a tiger spray marking. This was partly because the tiger was still primarily nocturnal and partly because the population in Ranthambhore was low enough for encounters between tigers to be infrequent. In the last twenty years, spraying has become normal activity throughout the year, especially after the monsoon, since the rain washes all these carefully placed scents away and a tiger has to mark his or her territory all over again.

Most tigers I have seen in Ranthambhore seem to prefer depositing their faeces on the central grass strip that runs down the middle of a road, or at the edge of a road or an animal path. They do not cover their faeces, but I have frequently observed scrape marks around the spot, as if the soil and grass have been raked. Sometimes defecation has taken place, in other cases urination, but at times the animal has simply left scrape marks. On five occasions, I have seen just a tiny sample of defecation on a raked patch, as if marking the spot; obviously this is yet another way in which tigers communicate their presence to others. They also rake their claws on the trunks of trees, which may again act as a territorial signal.

When Genghis was new to the area around Ranthambhore's lakes, he indulged in regular and incessant spray marking, tree clawing, soil scraping, defecation, and vocalization. On one walk around the lakes he covered a distance of 2 km in seventy-five minutes and spray marked eighteen trees, scraped the soil seven times, defecated once, and raked his claws on the bark of five trees. He also clutched the branches of two trees with his forepaws while standing on his hind legs. He was leaving every signal he could. This activity lessened markedly over the following months as he gained control of the area. When Kublai moved in, he did much the same through November and December but had eased off by March, by which time his presence was established.

Whether clawing, spraying, or scratching, most signals are left on the animal paths, nallahs (watercourses), and man-made roads that criss-cross the forest in Ranthambhore. This is probably because such belts and paths act as natural boundaries, demarcating ranges, especially for resident males. Specific trees in such areas are regularly sprayed and clawed, more so when a new tiger is asserting his rights.

Solitary or Not?

Tigers have long been thought to be solitary creatures, but twenty years ago two adult groups were very active in Ranthambhore. One of them consisted of two males and three females. One of the males was noticeably larger than the other, but the others were so similar in size that it was difficult to tell them apart. They could have been a family that never split up, although it would have been unusual for a tigress to raise a litter of five cubs to adulthood. Their general behaviour when hunting was not unlike that of a pride of lions. Around the meadows of the third lake, they would take different positions and lie in wait. If a deer came into the circle, one tiger would first stalk and then make a dash for it, pushing it toward one of the others, and in this way they would confuse the deer. I occasionally saw two of them, and on one occasion three, feeding together on the same carcass, but this is most unusual behaviour. I have seen tigers interacting over a kill only a few times, and Charles McDougal notes in his book *The Face of the Tiger* (1977) that on the fifty-nine occasions on which he observed tigers feeding on bait, he never once encountered two feeding at the same time.

The most exciting feeding behaviour I have seen in my life involved the tigress

Padmini and her cubs. One chilly November morning, I was driving when in the distance I saw a man on a bicycle gesticulating wildly as he approached. He shouted, 'There is a tree full of crows, and I have just seen a tiger feeding on a nilgai by Rajbagh.' I rushed to the tree he described, in which indeed fifty crows had perched. Below it sat Padmini with three fourteen-months-old cubs around her. Nearby lay the carcass of a huge bull nilgai, which must have weighed at least 250 kg, appreciably more than the tigress herself. It was far too heavy for Padmini to move, and she was nibbling at the rump, a small portion of which had already been eaten. The two cubs sitting behind her got up in an attempt to approach the kill, but she rose, coughed sharply, and slapped one of them across the face. The cub submitted, rolling over on its back, and settled down restlessly near her while the other cub started to eat from the rump. Padmini seemed to be dictating that the prey would be consumed one at a time.

Eventually, Padmini got up, grabbed the carcass by the neck, and tried to drag it away, but its foot got stuck in a forked tree root. She settled down to eat some more, and half an hour later tried again—this time dragging the carcass about 8 m. She then permitted the second cub to eat. A third cub waited some 30 m away.

Padmini then dragged the carcass about 10 m farther up the rise of a hill. I followed quickly and saw five tigers at different distances around the carcass, Padmini and Laxmi closest to it. Padmini got up, sniffed a tree, spray marked it, and walked toward her nearest cub, nuzzling it briefly. She then turned around and walked past Laxmi, snarling at her before grabbing the neck of the nilgai and pulling it farther up the hill.

A few minutes later, Padmini got up and walked down the slope of the hill toward the lake. Laxmi moved toward the carcass and started to feed. Surprisingly, I saw another adult tigress sitting nearby. It was Nick Ear, Padmini's daughter from her second litter. Padmini reappeared from the rear, marked a tree, and moved toward the kill. She and Laxmi coughed at each other. Padmini sat and snarled at Laxmi, who moved off toward Nick Ear and settled down on her side to sleep. Padmini also dozed off, but with a watchful eye on the crows perched on the branches. Then the dominant cub returned from the lakeside and sat at

the kill, nibbling at the fast-diminishing rump while Padmini watched alertly. By the end of the day, Padmini and her cubs, Laxmi, Nasty, Akbar, another of Padmini's offspring, and another tiger I couldn't identify—nine tigers in all—shared the kill.

I have never either witnessed or come across a description of another scene like this one, and I don't think one has been recorded in the wild before or since, anywhere in the world. I was sure that Padmini had made the kill but had decided to share the carcass with eight other tigers, two of whom were, so far as I knew, totally unrelated to her. And she was in complete control of the situation—not once did she permit two tigers to eat together, thereby obviating the conflict that could have arisen.

To find more than two tigers around a kill is a rarity. Nine was simply unbelievable. The fact that seven were related suggests the possibility of strong kinship links among tigers, sustained over long periods of time. I think that individual tigers do recognize one another. A great deal more of observation is needed to gather conclusive evidence on kinship links and their role, but this example shows that tigers can congregate without conflict around a kill—and with a female in charge of the feeding process.

From the summer of 1983 to early 1984, another group of tigers, also comprising two males and three females, roamed a similar area. The dominant member was a female who seemed to control the group's movements, and I observed them hunting on a number of occasions. But in February 1984, one of the males and one of the females disappeared. A month later, I found the surviving male and one female together and later discovered the second female with a gash on her rear flanks, presumably the result of a conflict within the group.

In both groups, the tigers remained together for varying periods, and their numbers changed due to conflict, which may have been caused by a tigress coming into estrus or by squabbles over food. Past observations of similar adult groups are quite illuminating. Edward B. Baker, a government officer serving in India, wrote in his book *Sport in Bengal* (1886): 'This animal is not the unsocial creature it is commonly understood to be. On the contrary, it is fond of consorting with others, and not seldom three or four may be found together; a mother and nearly full grown cubs; both parents and half grown ones; or a charming party of young males and females living and hunting together for a considerable length of time.'

But this sort of temporary association is the exception: it is very rare to find groups of tigers living together like lions. Except when a tigress has cubs, the long-held belief that tigers are basically solitary seems to be true.

Hunting

Cubs start to leave their mother when they are able to hunt successfully for themselves. Hunting is the most vital skill they learn from her; without this ability they have no chance of surviving as adults. Along with the need to reproduce, the search for food is the driving force of a tiger's life. Each tiger needs fifty deer-sized animals to eat each year—pretty much one per week—and of course a tigress with cubs needs more. Every animal killed necessitates a population ten times that in order for the species to remain sustainable. So fifty tigers need to kill a total of 2500 deer-sized animals per year, and an area that supports fifty tigers requires 25,000 such prey animals if the predators are to survive. In tropical forests like those in India, a carcass will be consumed in one to four days depending on its size, whereas in Siberia a kill may last up to a few weeks, since cold retards decomposition. Even in Siberia, however, there are few records in the wild of tigers coming back to eat their kills after about one week. A sambar deer, which can weigh 225–75 kg, will satisfy a large family. In the moist, deciduous forests of southern India, tigers can bring down an Indian ox or gaur weighing 550 kg and a large family will do well on this for more than a week.

One of the most interesting facets of how tigers hunt is that,

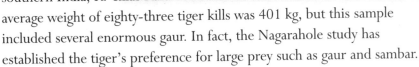

A tiger sits alert.

unlike many other predators, they do not seem to single out the young, the old, or the sick among their prey. George Schaller examined two hundred kills in the course of his study, and none of the prey was ill or suffering from injury. Mel Sunquist, studying tigers in Chitwan, reckons that 80 per cent of tiger kills weigh 50–100 kg, although adult male sambar are also taken. In Nagarahole National Park in southern India, K. Ullas Karanth noted that the average weight of eighty-three tiger kills was 401 kg, but this sample included several enormous gaur. In fact, the Nagarahole study has established the tiger's preference for large prey such as gaur and sambar.

I have watched tigers killing prey more than seventy times, and in my experience their hunting techniques vary tremendously depending on the individual and its mood. Tigers generally spend a fair amount of time patrolling their 'beats', mainly on man-made roads, on animal paths, or along streambeds. In between, they do a lot of sitting, watching, or sleeping, all of which conserve precious energy. Grooming is also an important activity, as the rasping tongue of the tiger flicks over every crevice and corner that it finds.

All this resting and grooming is done in a strategically placed day shelter where the tiger's senses will pick up any hint of prey. These shelters are generally in areas where deer graze, congregate, or are moving from one point to another. The tiger is a great observer of all the wildlife around it and a perfect opportunist. At the first suggestion of the presence of prey, the predator tends first to freeze, then to crouch and start a careful, silent, slow-motion movement toward its victim.

One morning, I encountered a tigress concealed in a patch of tall grass. She sat absolutely motionless, watching the movements of a small group of deer. At one point, she rose on her haunches and peered over the grass, checking her position in relation to the deer. Her stripes made her invisible, blurring any silhouette. They were the perfect camouflage.

A tiger peers out of the bush.

The tigress settled again, quite still. Unaware of danger, a sambar moved some 5 m toward her. She lifted her head. A quiver ran through her body, and then in a kind of slow motion she stalked forward a couple of metres with her belly touching the ground. The sambar looked up suspiciously, and the tigress dropped her head, completely concealed in the high grass. The sambar was now only 10 m away, but the tigress made no attempt to rush it. The light was low, but a tiger's eyes can detect any movement, as they concentrate available light on the retina, and the curve of the cornea creates wide-angle vision. They also provide binocular and 3-D vision. Tigers require only one-sixth of the light human eyes need in order to see.

The tiger moved a few metres with muscles bunched up. Its highly sensitive whiskers were nearly 15 cm long, circling the tiger's head and leading the way. Every time they touch an object, the tiger blinks in response and is thus alerted to what lies ahead. The sensitive touch of the padded paws also helps make the approach totally silent—avoiding even a dry leaf. Tigers creep, stalk, and walk on their toes.

Suddenly, the tigress stopped. Her tail twitched. It, too, is highly sensory. Even the hairs on the back of her forelegs are responsive to touch. A crested hawk eagle flew overhead. A couple of partridges scuttled away into a bush. A peacock cried in alarm. Soon, the sambar drifted away, and the chital moved off. The tigress's effort was in vain. She lifted her head for a moment, surveying the situation, then fell asleep in that position, her ears ever alert and responsive to sound. The deer had not spotted her. She stayed in the same patch of grass all day, waiting for the deer to drift close enough for her to launch her attack over a short distance. But they never did, and she had to wait until the next day to kill a young sambar and satisfy her hunger.

A second common hunting strategy is to take up a position near a water hole or grassy meadow and remain concealed, sometimes even asleep, until the unsuspecting deer move in closer. This is more prevalent during the summer, when the deer are forced toward water in large numbers—if a tiger remains undetected it will probably not move from its concealed spot all day.

It is an endless game of patience, with success depending on the wisdom and experience of the tiger. Sometimes one in ten attacks is successful, at other times one in fifteen. I once watched Nick Ear fail over and over again while trying out a new hunting technique.

One day I found her concealed in a bank of grass, carefully watching a sambar about 50 m away in the water. Shortly afterward, she came right out into the open and in slow motion covered the distance to the edge of the water one step at a time, freezing whenever the sambar glanced up. The confrontation between predator and prey was hypnotic. Just as Nick Ear reached the water's edge, one of the sambar hinds saw her and bellowed in alarm, and Nick Ear charged into the water, splashing and wading with powerful strides and then breaking into a swim. The sambar escaped out of the water, bellowing continuously. Nick Ear repeated this charge the next day at the same time, again unsuccessfully. Her careful stalk in the open, alternating between motion

A tiger chases into the water after sambar and targets a young fawn that is unable to move quickly enough against the water. One out of ten tries is successful in the water. This is a much better average than on dry land, where it is one out of fifteen or twenty.

and freezing, was immaculate, and the sambar remained undisturbed until she reached the lakeside. Only her lack of skill in attacking in water prevented her from succeeding.

One of the first natural kills I ever saw was from the balcony of Jogi Mahal, the forest rest house in Ranthambhore that overlooks one of the lakes. At 8:30 a.m., I had just returned from a morning drive. I decided to sit out on the balcony and have a cup of coffee. My gaze drifted to a group of fourteen chital grazing on the lush green grass at the edge of the lake. The coffee arrived, and I took my first sip, watching this serene lake and its surroundings. Then, quite unexpectedly, a cacophony of chital alarm calls drew my attention to a tiger who had charged the herd from the tall grass, startling them into confusion and successfully catching one.

The suddenness of the attack caught me by surprise. The next moment, the tiger gripped the neck of the chital and carried it off into the high grass around the lake. It looked as if it might be a doe.

Three other chital leaped in fright into the lake in an attempt to swim across to the far side. Within seconds, the first one vanished, followed rapidly by the other two—crocodiles having plucked them from under the water to gobble them up like chocolates. One tiger's attack had resulted in the death of four spotted deer.

The tiger's attack mechanisms are remarkable. The long leg bones above the knee joints provide leverage for handling heavy prey, while the extraordinary skeletal structure permits flexing, turning, twisting, and the rapid grasping of prey using the heavily muscled shoulders and forelimbs. This flexibility is particularly useful when dealing with large prey—a tiger learns from experience to avoid hooves, horns, antlers, even tusks if its intended victim is a wild boar. The thirty teeth are vital for killing and eating. The two upper canines can be 5–7.5 cm long, the lower two 4–5 cm; combined with the strong jaw muscles, they can deliver a lethal bite. With heavier prey, the aim is to force it down and then strangle

The chase continues. The tiger uses its powerful limbs more effectively in shallow water than the sambar can.

At times the tiger also brings down a gaur that can reach weights of 1000 kg.

it, basically crushing the windpipe. Smaller prey can often be dispatched with a single bite to the nape, which ruptures the neck vertebrae.

Stalking is a vital part of the tiger's hunting technique—the short lower limbs do not permit fast running, so the predator needs to be as close as possible to its prey before it is detected. Very seldom do you see the moment of impact when a tiger actually pounces on its prey. More often, you hear the kill and then come upon the aftermath. For human observers as for the animals themselves, ears are vital in a forest.

One day, while out scouting, I heard frantic chital calls and then a choked squeak. Convinced that it was the death cry of a chital, I moved to the spot. Just ahead, a tiger sat on its haunches, panting heavily. As I crossed a patch of grass, I encountered two more tigers. One was sitting with its paws hugging the carcass of a chital doe while the other watched alertly, moving a few steps forward. The first tiger emitted a low growl, and then with a loud 'woof' charged at the second. Both rose briefly onto their hind feet, 'mock boxing' each other, but soon the second one rolled over on its back as if in submission.

The second tigress eventually began to crawl toward the kill. Her head was close to the carcass and near the neck of the first tigress. The latter snarled viciously at her, but it had no effect. Amazingly, they sat like this, without eating, for thirty minutes. The growling, coughing, and snarling rose in a crescendo. I had never heard such a variety of tiger vocalizations before. It was aggression through sound, for at no time did the two animals attempt to injure each other.

Soon afterward, the first tigress relinquished her hold and sat at the rump to start feeding. The second immediately went to the neck and did the same. The dominant one plucked the tail of the carcass and spat it out. (Tigers in Ranthambhore tend to do this before eating from the rump.)

The two tigresses ate ferociously from either side of the carcass, the dominant animal keeping up a continuous low growl. I clearly saw her carnassial teeth slicing at the meat while the other molars and premolars gripped it. Her sharp claws were extended for grip and leverage—unsheathed they are a mind-boggling 11 cm long. Rough projections on the tongue also helped to remove hair and particles of meat. I have rarely seen two adults eating together. If a kill has to be shared, the subordinate tiger will normally wait its turn so that each eats alone.

As they ate, the tigresses' aggression manifested itself in great pulls from side to side, and after forty-five minutes the carcass appeared to be split down the middle, held together only by the skin. Eventually, it broke in two, the rump left with the dominant tigress and the neck, forelegs, and chest with the second. They both crunched on for another thirty minutes; intestines, rumen, and skin were all rapidly consumed.

In the late afternoon, this frantic eating was rudely interrupted by yet another tigress, who rose from a shady spot nearby and charged the two on the kill. To my surprise, the first two quickly dispersed, leaving

the remains to the newcomer, who immediately started feeding. I was sure she was the one I saw panting earlier, and think it likely that she killed the chital in the first place. However, she had permitted the other two females to eat before taking over. Most tigers in Ranthambhore are related in some way, which might explain this tolerance.

According to Charles McDougal, an adult tiger can consume 35 kg of meat at a single sitting. Mel Sunquist thinks the figure may be even higher. He argues that the maximum amount a tiger can eat in twenty-four hours is about one-fifth of its own body weight, which for a large male translates into 45 kg. I have seen a tiger consume an entire chital—about 30 kg of meat—at one meal.

I witnessed the incident described above because I had heard the sounds of the kill. The tiger does much the same thing. It is not only a master opportunist but also a great scavenger. It observes everything, following the alarms calls of sambar and chital or carefully watching vultures circling overhead and falling toward a kill. I have seen a tigress annexing a jackal's kill by tracing the movements of vultures in the sky. Tigers also respond to the sound of crows and magpies, the chatter of which leads them to the kills of other predators or to animals that have died of natural causes. There is a sense of inquiry

A tiger dragging a half-eaten carcass of a nilgai.

and investigation in the tiger as it roams the forest. I remember once hearing a distant wailing cry of a sambar. I had been watching a sleeping tigress, who awoke instantly at the sound and shot away like a bullet; within minutes, she was furiously charging some crocodiles that had captured a sambar fawn. On this occasion, she did not succeed in stealing the kill, but her ears had assessed the sound and dictated immediate action.

The way in which a tiger kills has long been a controversial subject among sportsmen and naturalists, and remains so among observers of the tiger today. This description, by Captain Thomas Williamson in *Oriental Field Sports* (1807), not only highlights the contempt in which tigers were held by early hunters but also shows that he had studied the tiger's hunting technique:

A tigress choking a langur monkey to death. Langurs only fall victim to tigers when they wander off from trees to the ground.

I have already observed that the tiger is of all beasts of prey the most cowardly, its treacherous disposition induces it, almost without exception, to conceal itself until its prey may arrive within reach of its spring, be its victim either bulky or diminutive. Size seems to occasion no deviation in the tiger's system of attack, which is founded on the art of surprising. We find, accordingly, that such as happen to keep the opposite side of a road, by which they are somewhat beyond the first spring, often escape injury, the tiger being unwilling to be seen before he is felt.

The tiger's forepaw is the invariable engine of destruction. Most persons imagine that if a tiger were deprived of his claws and teeth he would be rendered harmless, but this a gross error. The weight of limb is the real cause of the mischief, for the talons are rarely extended when a tiger seizes. The operation is similar to that of a hammer, the tiger raising his paw and bringing it down with such force as not only to stun a common sized bullock, or buffalos, but often crushing the bones of the skull.

Jim Corbett saw some twenty kills of tigers and leopards in his time. In one of these, a tiger made a head-on attack on a chital doe; otherwise, all the attacks were from the rear or at an angle. On one occasion when a tiger attacked a buffalo, the latter took off at full speed—with the tiger riding on its back. Eventually, the buffalo shook the tiger off and escaped, but not before the tiger had eaten some 2 kg of flesh from its withers and 5 or 6 more from its hindquarters. Corbett also recorded the killing of a very large elephant tusker by a pair of mating tigers, after a battle that lasted most of the night. While one leaped on the elephant's back, the other mauled its head.

Both Champion and Dunbar Brander point out that a tiger sometimes kills by dislocating its victims's neck and sometimes by strangulation. Hamstringing—severing the tendon at the back of the hock—is a technique used against very big prey. Only much later, once such an animal is down, will the tiger attempt to grip it by its neck. Sometimes it is not successful.

George Schaller once found a freshly killed chital doe with a lacerated throat and tooth punctures on the lower back, as if the tiger had tried everything before succeeding in killing it. He also recorded a sambar stag that was apparently straddled by a tiger and severely lacerated before it managed to escape with deep scars on its shoulders, side, and rump.

Traditional observation concludes that the tiger's primary method of killing is through a powerful wrenching grip on the neck that can crush the windpipe or neck vertebrae. Its eyes and whiskers function together, providing crucial information about where to deliver the lethal bite. Even the long canines are rich in pressure-sensitive nerves, enabling the tiger to hit the gaps between the bones of the neck, biting into and sometimes rupturing the spinal cord. But that is a generalization. In practice, the process of killing depends on the specific situation and the experience of the animal.

Special Hunting Techniques

I once had the extraordinary good fortune to encounter a tigress and her prey locked in struggle. For about twenty minutes I watched Noon, a tigress, trying and failing to kill a sambar.

I had returned from a morning drive, in the course of which I had had a brief glimpse of Noon and two cubs moving toward a dense area below the walls of the fort in Ranthambhore Park, presumably to lie up for the day. I was eating breakfast when a sambar alarm called twice. I left everything, grabbed the closest camera, and jumped into my jeep. In the clearing between the two lakes I found the three tigers moving toward Rajbagh. Noon had apparently changed her mind about her day shelter, for the group passed an old ruin that must have once been the entrance to a mosque. Now overgrown by grass and shrubs, it was one of Noon's regular day shelters.

Suddenly one of the largest sambar stags I have ever seen came galloping out of the area into which the tigers had disappeared. It was pursued closely by Noon. Stag and tigress disappeared from sight some 30 m ahead. After fumbling with the starter of the jeep, I moved ahead, my heart pounding. In a clearing a couple of metres from the vehicle track the stag stood motionless. Noon was clinging to the side of its neck. Her canines had a grip, but they were nowhere near the throat. Tiger and sambar were frozen in this position, staring at each other.

Because Noon's grip was on the side of the neck, she was unable to bring the sambar down or to suffocate it with the characteristic killing bite

of the big cats. She was going to have to use every hunting technique she had learned over the years. I took a few quick pictures, not sure how steady my hands were in the excitement of the moment. I decided to change position and moved up to within 3 m of them. They, too involved in their own struggle, were not in the least bothered by my presence.

After a few minutes, the sambar, with a great heave of his neck, shrugged the tigress off, but in a flash she attacked his forelegs. He jerked away, and Noon went again for the neck, rising on her haunches with one paw on his shoulder for leverage. The sambar swivelled around, so Noon had the chance to go for the belly and legs. After much struggling, the sambar found himself in a sitting position, with Noon keeping a firm grip on one of his hind legs. Noon's male cub appeared and stood motionless, observing the encounter. Noon and the sambar were again frozen in their positions. The cub inched closer, perhaps sensing victory. Noon yanked at the sambar's hind leg, opening the skin and trying desperately to break a bone. This was the only way she would be able to prevent him from escaping.

Suddenly, the sambar, utilizing every ounce of his strength, shook Noon off, stood up, and ran. The cub fled in fear, and an exhausted Noon tried to chase after her prey. The sambar, with a burst of adrenaline, escaped in the direction from which he had come. Noon loped after him but hadn't the energy to sustain any speed. The sambar gave his alarm call for the first time, a strange, dull, hollow sound, as if his vocal cords had been damaged in the attack. He waded into the lake, leaving Noon and her cubs watching from the shore. He stumbled

A tiger can run at speeds of up to 90 km an hour.

forward and found himself in a patch of
deep water; forced to swim, he nearly
drowned, his head bobbing up and down,
his limbs moving frantically as he struggled
to reach the far bank. The tigers followed
along the shore, but Noon soon gave up and
lay down, exhausted and panting. Her tongue
was cut and bleeding. The cubs jumped
around her, but she snarled again; getting the
message, they left her alone, moving off to
rest in the shade of a nearby bush.

The stag limped toward the shore and stood motionless for many
minutes in the shallow water. Noon watched for a bit but then decided
against pursuit—perhaps she simply didn't have the energy for another
battle. Instead, she walked away into dense cover to shelter, followed
by her cubs. The sambar slowly hobbled out of the water and onto a
bank of grass. His right foreleg looked twisted and broken; patches of
skin showed the raking marks of Noon's claws; and a bloody injury
swelled on the side of his neck. He died of his injuries a month later.

Noon rested for the remainder of the day, recovering from her
exertions, but managed to kill a different sambar stag the next day.
Predation is a complex art for which tigers evolve their own
techniques, which may vary according to seasonal changes and even to
the density of the habitat. Tigers commonly stalk prey stealthily for
up to 40 m, inching forward and using every available rock, tree, or
bush as cover to get as close as possible to their target before the final
charge, which could be from 3 to 9 m. In Ranthambhore, tigers have
also used jeeps as cover when stalking, and in the Russian Far East
they have used dense fog. Tigers in Ranthambhore's dry and open
habitat may develop hunting techniques very different from those
who inhabit the mangrove swamps at the edge of the Bay of Bengal.
There, the cover is so dense that a tiger is able to creep very close to
its prey before pouncing, so the prey has to deal with an almost
invisible predator. On the face of it, the Ranthambhore tigers have a
more difficult time, but on the other hand prey densities are much

A reflective retinal layer increases a tiger's ability to see at night at the expense of colour vision.

greater in Ranthambhore, so the odds are probably the same as anywhere else.

I witnessed one of the most fascinating hunting techniques for the first time when Genghis, who had established himself as the resident male, started to attack sambar in the shallow waters of the lakes. To me, Genghis was the great thinking tiger of Ranthambhore. On a typical day in the spring of 1984, I watched as Genghis moved into a patch of long grass after consuming the remains of a wild boar piglet he had killed the evening before. He slept in the shade of the grass until 2.30 p.m., when a group of sambar appeared on the shore and moved toward him. Genghis stood motionless in the tall grass at the edge of the lake, deciding which of the sambar to target. His eyes settled on one, and he started his charge, rushing diagonally through the grass toward it. The deer saw him, and with tails raised, calling in alarm, they fled farther into the lake. Genghis's diagonal run cut off any chance of the sambar escaping onto the shore, and they were forced into deeper water, confused and panic-stricken.

With a mighty leap, Genghis launched himself into the lake. The sambar frantically tried to flee, but the weight of the water hampered their movements. Crashing through the water amid sheets of spray, Genghis's power and speed were astonishing. He swerved toward his target, a young fawn, in an attempt to cut it off from the rest of the group. Its mother realized and turned in apparent anguish, knowing that her offspring had little hope of survival yet reluctant to desert it.

Genghis closed fast, pounding through the water with powerful strides. The sambar mother rushed away: she gave up, but from a safe distance she watched in distress. The tiger's paw smashed down on the helpless fawn with such force that fawn and tiger both disappeared beneath the water. Only Genghis's tail was visible. Beneath the water, his canines closed in a vise-like grip on the fawn's throat.

Genghis waded ashore, carrying the fawn in his mouth, flicking water from his tail as he headed for the cover of the grass thicket to feed in peace. The chase, from his emergence from the thicket to his disappearance back into it, lasted barely two minutes.

Genghis was a unique creature. I have never seen another tiger as powerful or as enterprising as he was. He ruled Ranthambhore's lakes for nine months then suddenly vanished, and I never saw him again. His hunting activity in the water remains unique in the body of tiger literature across the world.

Diet

The feeding behaviour of the tiger is also individualistic. Some tigers have been known to feed till the last morsel of meat is gone and to protect a kill with extraordinary ferocity even against crows and magpies. On the other hand, there are those who will eat what they can in their first sitting and then move on, leaving the leftovers to scavengers. I have seen tigers walk away from a kill even when hungry because they were weary of human disturbance. Some will allow humans to observe them at close quarters, while others are aggressive. Some will drag their kill to the thickest part of a forest to feed; others will happily feed in the open. A tiger, which itself weighs 110 to 220 kg, is capable of dragging a carcass weighing 180 to 225 kg up to 300 m. It yanks the kill in short bursts, either straddling it or pulling it in reverse. In Myanmar, formerly known as Burma, a tiger is said to have dragged a 770-kg gaur bull that thirteen men were unable to move even a metre. Lighter carcasses are often moved a few kilometres until a safe place can be found, especially if a tigress is carrying food to her cubs. She holds the prey in her mouth, and the limbs trail along the ground, leaving drag marks. Decades of observation reveal, however, that it is difficult to generalize about this or any aspect of tiger behaviour.

Smaller Prey

It is rare to see a tiger hunting smaller animals—the encounters tend to be quieter, for a start, so you have to be in the right spot at the right time.

Peafowl are well dispersed through the forest and can be found around bushy, grassy, and shrub areas, especially close to water. They play a vital role in helping humans pinpoint concealed tigers, mainly through two kinds of alarm—one when a bird watches a tiger at close quarters and shrieks its warning, the other when it takes flight after a close brush with a tiger. These alarms are also sounded if a peafowl spots a jungle cat, jackal, or bird of prey.

An adult male tiger guards the carcass of a sambar that he has appropriated from the resident female.

Three tigers and a peacock. Cubs learn the art of hunting by practising on peacocks, hares, and other small animals.

Twice when Laxmi and her family were walking through tall grass, I saw one of the cubs suddenly take off and leap into the grass. On the second occasion, this was followed by the shriek and death rattle of a peacock. I later had a fleeting glimpse of the cub as it bounded away, the peacock dangling from its mouth. I also once watched the amazing sight of a tigress with two cubs racing at full speed after a peacock who was frantically getting ready for flight, and on several occasions I have found the remains of a kill, with the peacock's exotic feathers scattered all over the place. As young tigers grow they chase everything in the bushes from quail to partridge and upward, and they regularly lie in wait for peafowl. For them, it is the first step in learning the art of killing and eating. Even adult tigers will pounce on or swat an unsuspecting peacock on the ground or on a low branch. The body contains 2–3 kg of meat, and it is likely that tigers look on it as a tasty snack.

Tigers also consume a variety of other birds and animals, in addition to the soil and grass that they munch with some regularity. H.R. Caldwell—an extraordinary character who was both a Christian missionary and a keen amateur naturalist working in China in the 1920s—reported cases of tigers eating pangolins (scaly anteaters). This has also been known in Bandhavgarh in central India. In Ranthambhore, I have twice seen remnants of monitor lizard in tiger scats.

George Schaller, in his study in Kanha, once spotted a tigress sitting alertly in tall grass; suddenly, she leaped high into the air to pounce on something, probably a rat or a mouse. Observers over the last century have discovered an enormous range of food items in the tiger's diet, including snakes, turtles, lizards, crocodiles, frogs, fish, and crabs—Schaller even found remains of winged termites and Sisyphus fruit in the droppings of a tiger. As long ago as 1886 Frank Simpson of the Bengal Civil Service wrote in *Letters on Sport in Eastern Bengal*, 'I have proved ... that [tigers] catch fish, turtles, corcodiles, and large lizards. I believe they will occasionally eat sugar cane and maize; but the most curious thing I ever knew them to eat was grasshoppers. I once killed a tiger whose paunch was crammed full of grasshoppers or locusts.'

Challenging Prey

The incident with Noon and the sambar is just one illustration of the difficulties entailed in hunting a powerful adversary. The Indian wild boar and the nilgai also present enormous challenges for the tiger. I remember late one evening hearing a ruckus in a field just outside the park. I rushed to the spot with a flashlight to find a tiger and wild boar facing each other. Amid snarls, roars, and grunts they charged each other, but in minutes the tiger was forced to flee. Only an experienced tiger or leopard would take on an adult boar. The male in particular, with his heavy body and fearsome tusks, poses a serious challenge.

Historical accounts leave no doubt that the boar is a courageous and daunting adversary for a tiger and that confrontations between the two are bloody and uncompromising affairs. In most encounters, the boar faces the tiger with hair and bristles erect, wheeling around with head lowered. The tiger, ears back and crouched low, circles the boar, then suddenly springs forward, attempting to strike a crippling blow with its paw. But the boar, even though squat and heavy, is very agile. It quickly exploits any weakness on the part of the tiger by charging with all its weight behind it, attempting to drive its tusks into the tiger's side or belly. The tiger tries to tear out chunks of flesh, but unless it is a really skilled hunter the boar is likely to wound or even disembowel it with its flashing tusks. One writer witnessed an incident in which even when dripping with blood and with bits of skin hanging from gaping wounds, the boar would not give up. Tiger and boar, bleeding, wounded, and exhausted, faced each other. The tiger was the first to limp off into thicker forest, followed by the boar. Both later died of their wounds.

On one occasion in Assam in the middle of the twentieth century, Patrick Hanley, the tea planter, observed a tiger preparing to spring on a group of wild boars when suddenly a chital let out its alarm call and the boars spotted the tiger. The adults instantly formed a protective screen

behind which the young ones scampered for shelter.
The tiger rose slowly, looked at them in
disgust, and sauntered off.

The wild buffalo is another
formidable adversary. Mike Birkhead
and I once filmed an incident in
Kaziranga, Assam, in which a buffalo
chased a tiger away. Seventy years
earlier, Victor Narayan witnessed a
remarkable encounter between the two
species in Cooch Behar in eastern India which
is recorded in *Thirty-Seven Years of Big Game
Shooting in Cooch Behar, the Duars, and Assam: A Rough Diary* by the
Maharajah of Cooch Behar (1908, reprinted in 1993):

The wild boar, a formidable adversary
of the tiger.

> He [Narayan] moved up to investigate, when to his astonishment he saw
> a magnificent bull buffalo moving along leisurely with on each side a tiger
> (probably tiger and tigress). Every now and then one tiger would dash in
> to try and get a hold, and the buffalo would merely sweep his horns. The
> tigers were evidently sparring for an opening. Neither the buffalo nor the
> tigers took any notice of the elephants which were following. This went on
> for about half a mile when suddenly one of the tigers got too close, and the
> buffalo immediately ripped it right up with his horns. The beast died at
> once. The other tiger bolted and the buffalo carried on unconcernedly.

The tiger is arguably the most powerful predator that walks the
earth. The only animal to which it has sometimes fallen prey in the
past is the dhole or wild dog. Packs of more than twenty dogs
surround a tiger and slowly tear it apart, even if losing several of
their number to the tiger's powerful swipes. W. Connell, writing in
the *Journal of the Bombay Natural History Society* in 1944, described
an occasion on which twenty-two wild dogs attacked a tiger. The
tiger killed twelve dogs but died in the process; the ten survivors
feasted on him.

Kenneth Anderson, who shot man-eaters during the 1940s and
1950s, witnessed an amazing battle between a pack of wild dogs and a
tigress that took place near Mysore in southern India:

The dogs had spread themselves around the tigress, who was growling ferociously. Every now and again one would then turn to attempt to rend asunder this puny aggressor, when a couple of others would rush in from another direction. In this way she was kept going continually, and I could see she was fast becoming spent. All this time the dogs were making a tremendous noise, the reason for which I soon came to know, when, in a lull in the fray, I heard the whistling cry of the main pack. The tigress must have also heard the sound, for in sudden, renewed fury she charged two of the dogs, one of which she caught a tremendous blow on its back with her paw, cracking its spine with the sharp report of a broken twig. The other just managed to leap out of danger. The tigress then followed up her momentary advantage by bounding away, to be immediately followed by the five remaining dogs. They were just out of sight when the main pack streamed by, in which I counted twenty-three dogs, as they galloped past me without the slightest interest in my presence.

The next day, Anderson's trackers returned with a few fragments of tiger skin. The dogs had cornered the tigress some 8 km away and torn her apart. Five dogs had been killed in the final fight.

Colonel Kesri Singh was the steward of Ranthambhore at the start of the twentieth century. He combined an uncanny ability to satisfy the maharajahs and foreign royalty who came to shoot there with an instinctive understanding that the area must not be over-exploited nor the tiger populations depleted. In his book *The Tiger of Rajasthan* (1959), he describes an evening he spent observing a tiger on a sambar carcass in the forest. He was able to watch it feeding for nearly thirty minutes. Suddenly, it looked up. In the distance, the cries of dholes echoed, and they seemed to be approaching. The tiger appeared anxious and uncomfortable but remained with its kill. Soon, the dogs arrived and surrounded the tiger, inching closer with loud cries. The tiger growled viciously, and the dogs whimpered. The tiger rushed at them, striking a couple with its paws, but then decided to flee through the opening it had made in the circle. Sacrificing its kill, it disappeared from sight, and the dogs tore at the carcass.

This description is all the more exciting because the dhole is no longer found in Ranthambhore. Or it wasn't until 1998, when a single animal appeared from nowhere. No one knows where it might have come from.

It is a male and seems to be still alive. Many people hope that a female will also stray in and that one day a pack will form.

Tigers and dholes tend to keep away from one another. The BBC television series *Land of the Tiger* includes footage shot in Kanha National Park in 1997 of a tigress chasing away a pack of dholes and appropriating their kill. Today, the wild dog is found only in small numbers, and large packs are rare. People, with their guns, are the only other predators the tiger needs to fear.

Interestingly, the tiger is potentially vulnerable to the defences of one of its smaller prey species, the porcupine. Scattered widely across India in open areas and grasslands, porcupines live in the earth or in rock crevices. They are great excavators, and in Ranthambhore are almost totally nocturnal. I have occasionally seen them rushing across the roads at night but never during the day. Porcupines weigh 12–16 kg, can reach lengths of 80–90 cm, live mainly on vegetables, fruits, and roots, and seem to have a good sense of smell. They defend themselves by charging backward with their quills erect, often also making a strange grunting sound.

I have on several occasions come across the scattered remnants of quills where a tiger has killed and eaten a porcupine, but I have never witnessed the kill itself. These quills are extremely sharp and can cause painful, sometimes fatal, injuries, so experienced tigers aim to effect a clean kill by striking or biting the porcupine's head, its most vulnerable spot. Amazingly, the tiger's intestine is tough enough to allow bits of porcupine quill to pass through it, but if it gets quills stuck in its paw it will try to pull them out. Often it will be successful and the wound will heal, but if the quills are deeply embedded, or if they are stuck in the neck, mouth, or jaw where they cannot be reached, the wound may turn septic. If this happens, the tiger is in constant pain and its hunting ability is seriously affected. It is forced to look for easier targets than its normal prey and so may

Tiger and porcupine. Sometimes porcupine quills inflict painful injuries around the tiger's mouth, neck, or jaw.

turn to cattle being grazed in the marginal parts of the forest. Jim Corbett describes a tigress who was seriously injured in an encounter with a porcupine and turned man-eater, killing twenty-four people before she herself was killed. Dead tigers have been found with quills embedded in their chests, paws, mouths, necks, and throats and even in the back of their heads. Corbett is said to have removed nearly two hundred quills from man-eaters he had shot, and some of these were up to 20 cm (almost 8 inches) in length. The porcupine is no easy prey, but tigers continue to relish it.

Unusual Prey

Tigers have a remarkably opportunistic diet. From Siberia comes an exceptional story of the tiger's approach to food. A seven-month-old tiger named Roma was captured after he attacked a person at a logging camp. Soon afterward, he was released several hundred kilometres away. Four months later, he was found roaming a forest looking thin and starved. The scientists who found him thought that as he had survived four months on his own he should be released again, but they radio-collared him so that they could keep track of his progress. Less than a month later, he was seen in a seal rookery along the coast, where he had killed and eaten seven seals. Hungry and weak though he was, he had found the seals easy prey. John Goodrich of the Siberian Tiger Project said of this, 'He didn't have a mother to teach him that seals are not normal tiger food! The seals, with their thick layer of energy-rich fat, gave Roma what he needed and when sighted by biologists a few months later in early spring, he appeared fat and healthy.'

Tigers have very rarely been known to kill langurs. It was my good fortune to witness this rare occurrence. I was watching Noon while she slept. Many hours had passed with little happening when suddenly I noticed a troop of langurs—the black-faced grey monkeys that inhabit much of the Indian subcontinent—behind her, jumping about in the branches of a tree and feeding on fruit. Noon briefly raised her head to watch them but then went back to sleep. After a few minutes, a large langur came out of the undergrowth as if to go toward the lake for water.

It was walking through tall grass, and I noticed it was getting very close to the tigress. Sure enough, it passed within 5 m of her.

Noon, disturbed by the rustling of the grass, awoke. Instantly, she spotted the langur and from a crouched position took one bound, followed by a flashing leap, and seemed to fall directly onto the defenceless monkey. For a crucial split second the langur was stunned, paralysed by this leaping apparition. Noon first pinioned it with her forepaws and then took a grip on its rear flank with her canines. The monkey shrieked and struggled furiously. Swiftly, Noon shifted her hold. Her canines closed on the neck, and in seconds the monkey was silenced. She now rose, holding the dead langur firmly by the neck, and stood still for some three minutes before moving off into the long grass to feed.

I had jumped onto the hood of the jeep to get a better angle from which to record this rare sight. Up in the trees, where they spend most of their time, langurs are safe from the tiger, but when they descend to the ground—and particularly when crossing open ground to drink at a water hole—they are very vulnerable. In this instance, the langur had been caught right in the open. As Noon fed, the rest of the langur troop climbed into a tree, gave a few sporadic alarm calls, and then sat in silence, as if uncertain what to do.

I soon left, only to find a large male langur striding down the road in the direction of the troop. My guess is that the dead langur was the dominant male and that this newcomer was from a nearby bachelor group.

The tiger is not the only predator that walks the forests of India. The leopard stalks the upper reaches, keeping as far away as it can from the tiger.

In Ranthambhore, we can actually see firsthand what the tiger eats. In addition, researchers can analyse material that tigers vomit—tiny bone splinters that lodge themselves in the stomach or digestive tract. In less open areas, observers have to rely on scat analysis, in which bits and pieces of prey and especially hair can provide detailed information.

In other parts of their range, tigers will also take livestock such as donkeys, goats, sheep, and even camels when the opportunity presents itself. Ranthambhore has known several instances of tigers attacking and eating camels around the fringes of the forest.

Tigers and Formidable Adversaries

On very rare occasions, tigers have been known to kill young elephants and rhinos and sometimes even bears and leopards. As far as elephants are concerned, probably the most amazing story comes from E.A. Smythies, a forest officer who observed this incident near the Sarda River in Uttar Pradesh, northern India, in 1940:

Late one evening in the last week of September, three men were fishing with nets in the waters of the Sarda, two or three furlongs from the bungalows on the bluff, when suddenly two tigers and a half-grown cub emerged from one of the grassy islands close by. The men shouted and yelled until the tigers moved off across the dry bed of the river toward the forest on the right bank, a quarter of a mile away upstream from the trumpeting of a wild elephant. Shortly afterwards the fishermen, and the few dozen inhabitants of the bazaar, heard the nerve-shattering roar of a charging tiger, and the fishermen saw a big male tusker elephant come out into the open river bed, being attacked by the two tigers. For three hours the battle between the elephant and the tigers raged up and down the river bed, below the high bluff, in full moonlit view of the bungalows on the cliff. Would that I had been there to see and hear! The bazaar inhabitants were so terrified at the appalling noise and infuriated roars of the tigers close at hand, that they barricaded themselves in their houses and no one, except the petrified fishermen who were cut off, saw this awe-inspiring and unique spectacle. At about 11 p.m. the noise died down, and by next morning the tigers had departed, but the dead elephant was lying at the foot of the bluff, within a stone's throw of a bungalow.

Some records from the early twentieth century contain accounts of tigers killing and eating leopards, especially in battles over kills. Even recently in Corbett National Park a tiger fought and killed a leopard and proceeded to eat it. There have been similar reports from elsewhere in India, which help to explain why leopards keep away from tigers. In Ranthambhore and Kanha National Parks, tigers have been known to 'tree' leopards and keep them there for several hours. K. Ullas Karanth describes an encounter between a tiger and a leopard in Nagarahole National Park whose purpose seems to have been to teach the leopard his place.

TIGERS AND LEOPARDS
K. Ullas Karanth

It was 10:00 a.m. The sun was getting unpleasantly hot in my open jeep parked alongside a game road in southern India's Nagarahole National Park. I had been radio-tracking Sundari, a 145-kg beauty of a tigress, since dawn. In fact, I had been studying her for almost exactly three years to that day in 1993. Her inactive radio signals indicated that she was resting in a nearby shady forest patch of dense lantana, bamboo, and scattered trees. Speculating that she was unlikely to stir until late that evening, I drove back to the field camp for a quick breakfast.

When I returned a mere half hour later, Sundari's signals were emerging from across the road. She had moved about 200 m, disturbed or attracted by some event. I decided to investigate by calling in my most versatile all-terrain vehicle: a riding elephant named Kalpana, with her mahout, Kariya. Although the thick-skinned beast pushed through thorny bamboos with silky smoothness, riding on her back Kariya and I were clawed relentlessly by them. The signals drew us to the base of a 15-m-tall *lagerstroemia* tree.

As we got closer, an extraordinary sight greeted us: perched precariously on the *lagerstroemia*, looking down and growling hideously in fear, was a big male leopard. We could see Sundari's striped hide.

I knew her fearsome canines could snap the 60-kg leopard's neck like a matchstick if she caught him.

As we drew closer, the leopard grew increasingly nervous: he did not like being forced to choose between this lumbering pachyderm and the silent assassin below. Jumping off his perch, he made a sudden dash for safety. Sundari was after him like a rocket. Fierce growls rent the air as the two big cats grappled in a struggle that lasted barely twenty seconds. Evading Sundari's clutches, the leopard raced back up the tree with an agility unimaginable in a creature its size. Sundari charged at the tree, trying to grab him. She missed, and her bulky form slid down the tree trunk. She made one more futile attempt, reaching about 5 m high before sliding down. By then, the leopard had reached the top and found a safe perch. He sat there, bobbing and glaring sullenly at the tigress and at us. Gradually, his growls subsided. In a few minutes, radio signals emerging from the dense cover told me that Sundari, too, had gone to sleep somewhere close by, in case the leopard made a move again. We withdrew some distance away to make sure he did not.

The scorching sun rose in the sky and then slid slowly to the western horizon. I kept up the vigil, with the two big cats frozen in their respective positions. By 6.45 p.m., it was pitch dark and time to head back to camp. Although I could still hear Sundari's signals, I could not see anything.

I returned to the spot at daybreak. Sundari's distant signals told me she was rapidly moving away. I feared the worst for the leopard as a crow flew off from beneath the *lagerstroemia* with a piece of red, raw meat in its mouth. However, a closer look led me to the pitiful remains of a sambar fawn.

The leopard had apparently killed the fawn the previous morning, after I left for breakfast. Attracted by the deer's distress calls, Sundari had come to investigate, forcing the panicky leopard up the tree, just before I returned. Having waited in ambush through the night, the tigress had given up and walked away earlier in the morning. In his hurry to escape, the leopard had even left uneaten what remained of his hard-earned kill. Here was living proof of the social domination that the larger-sized carnivores usually exercise over their smaller cousins.

K. Ullas Karanth has studied tigers for twenty years. He earned his doctorate in wildlife biology with a focus on predator-prey relationships in Nagarahole National Park in southern India.

In Chitwan, Charles McDougal recorded five leopards killed by tigers over a period of twenty-one months. In one instance, a female with two cubs was attacked by a tigress who killed and ate the mother, leaving only the head and front paws. The two cubs escaped but returned to the area the next night only to be killed by the tigress, whose own cubs, aged six months, dragged the small corpses around.

Tiger and crocodile were first seen coming into conflict in Ranthambhore in Genghis's time—even when he wasn't hunting for himself he would charge into the water, snarl ferociously at crocodiles feasting on a sambar carcass, and literally yank it away, splashing at the crocodiles with his huge paws.

Fateh Singh Rathore has recorded an instance of a tiger–crocodile conflict in Ranthambhore.

TIGER–CROCODILE FIGHT
Fateh Singh Rathore

In November 2002, I was driving in the park along the road behind the rest house when I heard a sambar call. I drove fast and found that the resident tigress had killed a sambar in thick bushes and was sitting on its neck. She had to rest for a while, as tigers become breathless after a kill.

Later, she went to fetch her cubs from the other side of Jogi Mahal. On her return, she found a large crocodile feasting on her kill. She was furious and rushed at it, roaring loudly; the crocodile responded with a loud snapping of its jaws. The tigress tried to topple it off the kill, but every time it regained its normal position and hit out at her, lashing its tail vigorously. Then the tigress managed to straddle the crocodile's neck, struggling to bite the joint between head and shoulder. She bit off a piece of skin before the crocodile shook itself free and moved off toward the lake; the tigress then dragged the sambar across the road, where the cubs started eating. They had been watching from a safe distance and seemed quite excited while the fight was going on.

Early the next morning, I found that the sambar kill had been dragged about fifty metres into the ruins of the fort. I could see the tigress's face in the shadows. The crocodile was still lying where I had last seen it, at the side of the lake. I thought it was dead. At 10.30 a.m., three village dogs appeared—they must have thought the crocodile was dead, too, because they started feeding on it, but then it got up and dragged itself to the water. The dogs were quite taken aback, and after two more attacks they gave up and ran away.

Meanwhile, the tigress had been watching all that was happening. She dashed from cover, grabbed the crocodile by the tail as it struggled toward the comparative safety of the water, and turned it around so that it was facing away from the lake and toward the jungle. It must have been weak and disoriented, because it stayed there all day. The tigress returned to her sambar kill. At about five o'clock she called her cubs, who appeared from the nearby bushes. She left them feeding on the sambar while she went down to the lake to drink. As she passed the crocodile she tried to step on its back, but it shook her off, moving just a little and wagging its tail. On her way back, she ignored the crocodile completely and returned to her cubs, who were waiting in the road.

The next day the crocodile died.

Fateh Singh Rathore was the field director of Ranthambhore National Park from 1979 to 1987. He has spent 40 years working with wild tigers, and continues to live near the park.

Instances of tigers eating another reptile—the huge Indian python, which can attain a length of 4 m—have been recorded in Dudhwa on the India–Nepal border and in Bandhavgarh in central India. If the python happens to be constricting a small deer, the tiger is able to chew on both!

One of the most exciting incidents I have found in the thousands of pages written on tiger hunting in India comes from Colonel F.W.T. Pollok in *Incidents of Foreign Sport and Travel* (1894). He was up a tree on a machan, waiting to shoot a man-eating tiger near the corpse of one of its victims:

I do not think I could have borne the gruesome sight much longer, when there was a roar, and a brindled mass sprang at something which was

An extremely rare occurrence: a tiger attacking an enormous crocodile, unusual prey for the tiger.

invisible to me. Instantaneously a vast speckled body coiled itself round the brindled matter, there was a struggle, bones seemed to be crunched to bits, the tiger gave a feeble roar or two, and then all was still except an occasional convulsive up-heaving.... That long, long night at length terminated, and thankful I was to see the dawn of day and hear the jungle fowls proclaim that sunrise was at hand—losing no time I descended to solve last night's mystery. The sight that met my eyes was marvellous. A huge rock snake, a python, just over twenty-one feet in length, lay coiled round the body of the tiger whose fangs in turn were embedded in the back of the snake's head, while the reptile's folds, after enveloping the tiger, had got a purchase by lashing its tail round the adjoining sapling, and so assisted the vast muscular power it possessed in crushing the tiger to death.

Fateh Singh Rathore writes of confrontations between sloth bears and tigers in Ranthambhore.

SLOTH BEAR AND TIGER CONFLICT
Fateh Singh Rathore

I have seen sloth bears many times, digging in termite mounds; quite often a tiger will pass by, and the two creatures will ignore each other. But in April 2001, I saw a tigress, who I knew had young cubs, charging a sloth bear. A few weeks later, the same tigress left her sambar kill to stalk slowly toward a sloth bear that was feeding on the fruits of a nearby tendu tree. The bear came down from the tree and charged her. It was a kind of hide-and-seek for fifteen minutes until the sloth bear left the area. It is possible that the bear was trying to approach the kill, and that the tigress was trying to divert it on behalf of her cubs.

In December 2002, I watched a sloth bear approach the Sakari water hole. A young male tiger was also watching from the bushes. After drinking the bear moved toward a ber tree, which he shook in order to dislodge its fruit. As he fed, the tiger crept up on him, unable to charge because of the long grass. After almost half an hour, the bear turned on the tiger. Both tiger and bear stood on their hind legs and tried to hit each other. This happened three times; then the tiger retreated a few metres, and the bear, unperturbed, wandered off. A few metres away, another tiger, the brother of the first, appeared in front of the bear but did not attack or approach him. The bear simply walked past. The second tiger joined his brother, and the incident was over.

Two months later, on 13 February 2003, a sloth bear and two tigers again came face to face. The tigers had killed a sambar near the Sakari water hole. They were both drinking when the sloth bear appeared. They turned on him aggressively, but he seemed indifferent to them. Totally relaxed, he approached the water, drank, and moved off toward the tigers' kill. The tigers also returned to the kill; one of them tried to attack the bear, roaring loudly, but the bear turned on him and charged, also roaring. Once the tiger had retreated, the bear returned to the kill and continued to feed. Only one tiger attempted to attack the bear; the other sat watching. Over the next thirty minutes, the first tiger approached a number of times, but the bear simply ignored him.

In Ranthambhore, tigers do not seem to be interested in killing sloth bears, although the bears often appropriate their kills; perhaps they have never learned from their mothers to kill bears nor seen her doing so. In many other places, there is evidence that tigers have killed sloth bears in the presence of cubs, so the cubs grow up knowing that this is a prey species and not a competitor to be feared. Later, on 10 March I found a drag mark and lots of bear hairs. Looking around, I found tiger pugmarks but no bear carcass. It seems likely that the mother of the two cubs killed the bear, and I have not seen a sloth bear in the area since.

Courtship and Mating

Adult life for wild tigers is about hunting and reproduction. Real adulthood begins with the ability to reproduce. For females, it is between the ages of twenty-eight and thirty-six months when they first come into estrus and are able to conceive; for males it is later, forty to fifty months, when they are able to father a litter.

The process of courtship and mating starts with the tigress coming into estrus, and on the three occasions on which I have witnessed this stage the behaviour pattern has been identical. The tigress becomes restless, vocal, and very mobile. My first encounter proved to be typical. Early one morning, I was listening intently for sounds of alarm in the forest when I heard a long moan, repeated at regular intervals. I followed the sound and found a tigress walking down the road. In the forty-five minutes that I kept pace behind her, she vocalized some thirty times and spray marked trees or rubbed herself on the bushes some twenty-five times. The forest echoed with her wails—peacocks flew off in alarm, and at one time a group of sambar bellowed at her in panic before fleeing. She was completely unconcerned and walked along briskly, stopping to spray a tree or rub her haunches on patches of grass or bush. Sometimes she would rub her neck high against the trunk of a tree. I was mesmerized by her total obsession with her physical condition. She was using all her energies to call and mark so as to attract any male in the vicinity. Even if one did not pass through the area until later, he would be able to smell her scent and follow her. Eventually, I lost sight of her as she disappeared into a thick ravine.

Sometimes a tigress's intense marking and calling will attract a single male. On other occasions, more than one will appear, and then a vicious fight may break out. Patrick Hanley recorded an instance when he found a tigress calling with great regularity. This soon attracted a male tiger who cautiously started his approach, but before he could reach her another male arrived and promptly attacked the first. The two tigers

Sloth bears share this land of the tiger, and frequently chase away tigers that they encounter.

seem to have wrestled on their hind legs, clawing and attempting to bite each other and roaring viciously. One of them succeeded in tearing the other's neck open with a slash of its claws. The battle was savage, and one of the tigers soon departed from the fray, bleeding and limping badly.

Hanley then observed a third male watching from behind a bush. The victor of the recent fight had a great weal across his ribs where he had been torn by his opponent's claws. He rolled around in a patch of grass, wiping the blood away, and then approached the tigress. As he came to within a few paces of her, the third male sprang toward him. The exhausted victor was no match for the third tiger and was easily chased away. Soon, the tigress and the third male bounded away into the forest. The tigress had sat quietly throughout, observing the aggressive conflict over her.

Fateh Singh Rathore had a once-in-a-lifetime experience observing mating tigers, which he described in detail to me. On a spring morning the sky was dark and stormy. A sambar carcass was floating in one of the pools, but there were no signs of tigers. Satisfied that Kublai and Noon were not in the immediate area, Fateh drove back to the rest house, content to try again later. At four in the afternoon, a radio message came through, telling of alarm calls in the area of Rajbagh. Fateh rushed back to the lake and to the small pool where the carcass was still lying. By then, a gale was blowing. Covered with a film of dust, Fateh sought the shelter of some trees.

At 5:20 p.m., Noon emerged from a thicket of grass and sat at the edge. She was soon followed by Kublai, who reclined some metres away. Both tigers appeared relaxed. Suddenly, Noon rose and strode rapidly over to Kublai, who raised his head. Noon rubbed her flank against him. He rose, and she quickly settled in front of him, offering him her rear quarters. Immediately, Kublai mounted her, and some fifteen seconds later Noon growled sharply, followed by a few lower-pitched growls, which lasted another ten seconds. Then Kublai jumped off, and Noon, after a sharp grunt, stood up and moved away. They both lay down to rest. Eleven minutes later, Noon rose again and moved quickly toward Kublai, seductively rubbing her head and her right flank against his mouth. She then sat in front of him. Kublai stood again and mounted her. This time, they were partially hidden by the grass thicket. Noon emitted a sharp grunt, and after thirty seconds Kublai jumped off.

Then Kublai moved right out of the grass and slowly walked around the edge of the lake. He paused to stretch himself on the fallen trunk of a palm tree and then walked on the trunk before moving to the edge of the water, close to the sambar carcass. He snarled viciously at a couple of corcodiles attempting to nibble at the carcass and settled down to watch against a backdrop of a red flowering tree, the 'flame of the forest', with the flowers scattered around him on the grass. Fateh, watching from the other side of the pool, was astonished at the raw beauty of the scene. Tiger, red flowers, and sambar carcass were all reflected in the water, creating images of poetic intensity.

Noon quickly followed Kublai's path to the edge of the water. With a sharp snarl at a gliding crocodile she encouraged a response from Kublai by nuzzling him, sliding her flank against his, and then sitting receptively at the edge of the water less than a metre in front of him. Kublai rose, seemingly aroused again by Noon's provocative position. He mounted her, sliding his forepaws down her back until they made contact with the ground near her forelegs. His head leaned against the side of her neck, as if they were entwined. His hind legs remained half bent as his forelegs straddled Noon's neck. Her forelegs were fully stretched and the hind legs slightly bent. After fifteen seconds, she again emitted a sharp growl, and Kublai gripped the folds of skin around the nape of her neck. Some seconds later, she threw him off, snarling aggressively. Carefully, they each licked every inch of their rears, especially their genitals. Fifteen

The huge Indian rock python also forms a part of the tiger's diet.

minutes later, Noon initiated another session of copulation in much the same way.

The sun had set and the forest sounds had changed as the crickets took over. Way out in the distance, a brown fishing owl flew off in search of prey, and a pair of golden orioles flitted across the sky, the bright yellow of their chests providing relief against a dull forest green.

Then Noon walked off around the edge of the lake. Kublai followed, but he had gone only a few metres when the crocodiles returned to the carcass, and he decided to retrace his steps. Amid much snarling, he settled down at the edge of the water, looking carefully at the carcass some 3–4 m away. Noon was out of sight. After five minutes Kublai rose again as if to follow her, but the crocodile activity again forced him to retrace his steps. He seemed caught between staying around the carcass and being with Noon. The light slowly faded. Minutes later, Noon returned; again she rubbed bodies with Kublai, and they mated.

Kublai's interest in the sambar carcass was much greater than Noon's—she seemed not in the least bothered about food. In the next half hour, the two tigers mated three more times. Their perfect reflections glinted off the water. Night slowly took over. Fateh had watched eight copulations in eighty-eight minutes. It had been his most exciting observation ever of tiger behaviour. Awed by the power and beauty of the scene, he drove slowly back to Jogi Mahal.

The next day, there was no trace of the tigers. The saga was over. Thirty-five days of regular interaction had finally culminated in the mating of Kublai and Noon.

Observations of mating are rare and very seldom recorded. Tigers obviously prefer privacy, free from the disturbance of humans, but we know that mating couples may spend two to four days together. A tigress who conceives may not come into estrus again for eighteen to twenty-two months, though there are exceptions to this. Very little information is available on the tiger estrus cycle in the wild, but zoo records show that tigresses who do not conceive—or who lose their litters for some reason—will come into estrus again anywhere from one to three months later. Like other cats, tigers are induced ovulators—the female releases an egg only once mating has begun. This helps to ensure that a female in

A tragic day in the 1980s when three nine-month-old cubs were killed by a territorial male tiger in Ranthambhore.

estrus finds a male before she is actually ready to conceive, increasing the chances of her becoming pregnant when she mates. The penis bone (in the male tiger, an actual bone) stimulates the tigress, inducing ovulation.

A male tiger may be capable of mating and fathering cubs before he reaches the age of four to five years, but he seldom gets the chance. By that age, he is in his prime, strong enough to have taken over a territory and protect the females that go with it. Yet his active reproductive life will probably last only a few years before he is ousted by a younger male. The reign of one male tiger in Chitwan lasted only four years, but he had seven females in his territory and succeeded in siring twenty-seven cubs in that time. In zoos, a tiger may survive to the age of twenty-six, and age twenty is not uncommon. A captive female has been known to give birth at seventeen. But in the wild, a female does well to live and breed until the age of fourteen or fifteen. Most male tigers fare rather worse, dying by the age of ten or even younger because of the frequent territorial struggles they must endure. But much remains to be discovered on this subject, as the body of a dead tiger is rarely found in the wild—the tiger is as evasive in death as it often is in life.

Let us end this account of the life of the Bengal tiger with an extract from the bitter-sweet tale of a magnificent specimen—the Pipal Pani Tiger—whom Corbett had tracked for fifteen years before shooting him in the mistaken belief that a gun wound he had received was serious enough to turn him into a man-eater.

THE PIPAL PANI TIGER
Jim Corbett

He was about a year old when, attracted by the calling of a chital hind early one November morning, I found his pugmarks in the sandy bed of the little stream known locally as Pipal Pani. I thought at first that he had strayed from his mother's care, but, as week succeeded week and his single tracks showed on the game paths of the forest, I came to the conclusion that the near approach of the breeding season was an all-sufficient reason for his being alone. Jealously guarded one day, protected at the cost of the parent life if necessary, and set adrift the next, is the lot of all jungle folk; nature's method of preventing inbreeding.

The winter he lived on a peafowl, kakar, small pig and an occasional chital hind, making his home in a prostrate giant of the forest felled for no apparent reason, and hollowed out by times and porcupines. Here he brought most of his kills, basking, when the days were cold, on the smooth bole of the tree, where many a leopard had basked before him. …

The following winter I saw him several times. His ears did not look so big now and he had changed his baby hair for a coat of rich tawny red with well-defined stripes. The hollow tree had been given up to its rightful owners, a pair of leopards, new quarters found in a thick belt of scrub skirting the foothills, and young sambar added to his menu.

On my annual descent from the hills next winter, the familiar pugmarks no longer showed on the game paths and at the drinking places, and for several weeks I thought the cub had abandoned his old haunts and gone farther afield. Then one morning his absence was explained for, side by side with his tracks, were the smaller and more elongated tracks of the mate he had gone to find. …

A week later the tiger resumed his bachelor existence. A change had now come over his nature. Hitherto he had not objected to my visiting his kills but, after his mate left, at the first drag I followed up I was given very clearly to understand that no liberties would in future be permitted. The angry growl of a tiger at close quarters, than which there is no more terrifying sound in the jungle, has to be heard to be appreciated.

Early in March the tiger killed his first full-grown buffalo. I was near the foothills one evening when the agonized bellowing of a buffalo, mingled with the angry roar of a tiger, rang through the forest. ...

Three years later the tiger ... incautiously returned to a kill, over which a zamindar and some of his tenants were sitting at night, and received a bullet in the shoulder which fractured the bone. ...

When we came down from the hills two months later the tiger was living on small animals (calves, sheep, goats, etc.) that he was able to catch on the outskirts of the village. By March his wound had healed, leaving his right foot turned inwards. Returning to the forest where he had been wounded, he levied heavy toll on the village cattle, taking, for safety's sake, but one meal off each and in this way killing five times as many as he would ordinarily have done. The zamindar, who had wounded him and who had a herd of some four hundred head of cows and buffaloes, was the chief sufferer.

In the succeeding years he gained as much in size as in reputation, and many were the attempts made by sportsmen, and others, to bag him.

One November evening, a villager, armed with a single-barrel muzzle-loading gun, set out to try to bag a pig, selecting for his ground machan an isolated bush growing in a twenty-yard-wide rowkah (dry watercourse) running down the centre of some broken ground. ... At 8 p.m. an animal appeared on the track and, taking what aim he could, he fired. On receiving that shot the animal fell off the bank, and passed within a few feet of the man, grunting as it entered the scrub behind. ...

Arrived at the spot where the animal had entered the bushes, a careful search was made and, on blood being found, every effort to find the 'pig' was made; it was not until the whole area had been

combed out that the quest for that night was finally abandoned. Early next morning the search was resumed ... [and] examining the ground under a bush where there was a lot of blood, [one of my tenants] collected and brought some blood-stained hairs to me which I recognized as tiger's hairs. ...

There was no blood beyond the point where the hairs had been found and, as tracking on the hard ground was impossible, I crossed the canal to where the cattle track ran through a bed of sand. Here from the pugmarks I found that the wounded animal was not a young tiger as I had assumed, but my old friend the Pipal Pani tiger who, when taking a short cut through the village, had in the dark been mistaken for a pig.

Once before when badly wounded he had passed through the settlement without harming man or beast, but he was older now, and if driven by pain and hunger might do considerable damage. A disconcerting prospect, for the locality was thickly populated, and I was due to leave within the week, to keep an engagement that could not be put off. [After four days of searching, Corbett eventually managed to track down the tiger and shoot him.]

After the impact of the heavy bullet, he struggled to his feet and tore blindly through the forest, coming down with a crash within a few yards of where, attracted by the calling of a chital hind one November morning, I had first seen his pugmarks.

It was only then that I found he had been shot under a misapprehension, for the wound which I feared might make him dangerous proved on examination to be almost healed and caused by a pellet of lead having severed a small vein in his right forearm.

Pleasure at having secured a magnificent trophy—he measured 10 ft 3 in over curves, and his winter coat was in perfect condition—was not unmixed with regret, for never again would the jungle folk and I listen with bated breath to his deep-throated call resounding through the foothills, and never again would his familiar pugmarks show on the game paths that he and I had trodden for fifteen years.

Jim Corbett, India's most famous hunter of man-eaters, was a pioneer in many respects—a hunter par excellence with over a dozen man-eaters (thought to have taken more than 1500 lives) to his name, and a committed conservationist who helped establish India's first national park, subsequently named after him. This extract has been taken from the story 'The Pipal Pani Tiger' included in *Man-eaters of Kumaon*, first published in 1944.

The Future of the Tiger

The Vanished Cult of the Tiger

Ancient Indian and South Asian history and legend is, of course, full of references to tigers, but an enormous cult of the tiger arose across the rest of Asia as well, including even parts of Siberia. Across its entire range, the tiger became an integral part of the life of the traditional communities, and its widespread influence on religious cults and legends, on art and literature, and on the way of life was unmatched by any other non-domesticated animal. Wherever it existed, it left its impress on the psyche of the people. The Warli tribal peoples of India believed that the tiger was the greatest of all gods and that all other gods existed because of him. Phallus-shaped wooden and stone images of the tiger, often daubed in red to indicate their extreme sanctity, were placed everywhere as symbols of fertility, not just for crops but also for marriage and the birth of children. There were festivals dedicated to the tiger god all across India, and there were ritualistic dances in which dancers painted themselves with tiger stripes and then propitiated the tiger god. The tiger commanded great respect across different religions. Buddhist texts contain the legend of the compassionate prince giving his body to save the life of a starving tigress and her cubs.

Thousands of miles away in Siberia, the Udege tribal peoples also honoured the tiger as their god. To the Udege, the tiger is the spirit of the taiga (evergreen forests) and guardian of the trees and mountains, a

An eighteen-month-old cub folds its massive paws as it sprawls on the ground.

divine force of nature. Similarly, many Koreans still believe that their land is blessed by the blue dragon and the white tiger, and that the image of the tiger repels evil spirits and protects people's fortunes. Much the same was felt in China. Many believe that the tiger first originated in China and then spread across Asia. At one time, most Chinese believed that the breath of the tiger created wind. Edward Schafer in his book *The Vermilion Bird* (1967) states, 'Chinese literature from the earliest times is full of tiger stories—man-eating tigers, were-tigers, symbolic tigers, anti-tiger spells, tiger hunts—tigers in China are like mice in a cheese factory.' Three thousand years ago, during the Shang Dynasty, people in the Shaanxi province believed that the tiger symbolized regeneration. A bride would receive two dough tigers when she first arrived at her husband's house (a tradition that continues to this day). In Chinese medicine, the body of the tiger is believed to hold miraculous cures.

It is notable that among all the communities that shared the forest with the tiger, it was never feared as a bloodthirsty, mindless killer; rather it enjoyed a sacred status as protector of the forests. Never was the tiger wantonly killed, and elaborate codes guarded all game for the people who greatly depended on it for their livelihood. Before the advent of the European with his gun, his search for manhood-affirming trophies, and his irrational fear of the tiger, the tiger was indeed king of his jungles. Man and tiger lived together in harmony, and although tiger killing formed an important part of the ceremonial of forest communities, elaborate taboos surrounded its killing for any purpose other than the ceremonial. Even with the early advent of trophy-hunting, wantonly killing Europeans, anyone who transgressed these codes by acting as tiger guides to the Europeans faced excommunication. For India, writing in the early twentieth century, hunter and forester A.A. Durbar Brander records:

> At one time in parts of India at the beginning of the last century, they [tigers] were so numerous it seemed to be a question as to whether man or tiger would survive.
>
> Up till about the beginning of the present century, sportsmen only visited the Central Provinces in moderate number, but about this time shooting became a popular pastime amongst army officers and tigers were much reduced. ... Few tigers are killed by native shikaris. ... It is the European sportsmen that thins out the tiger.

Thus it is only with the slow dying out of traditional ways of life of the forest people in the face of the relentless march of civilization that the tiger faces a threat.

Extinct Tigers

The world's current population of tigers represents only five of the original eight subspecies into which the tiger was divided: the Amur (*Panthera tigris altaica*), the Bengal (*Panthera tigris tigris*), the Indo-Chinese (*Panthera tigris corbetti*), the South China (*Panthera tigris amoyensis*), and the Sumatran (*Panthera tigris sumatrae*) tigers. The first four are now classified as the Asian tiger (*Panthera tigris tigris*), the last as the Sunda Island tiger (*Panthera tigris sondaica*). In fact, no South China tigers have been seen in the wild since the 1980s, although there are records of pugmarks and of prey killed by tigers. They may already be extinct, or a few may still be roaming the forests. The last 100 years have seen enormous damage.

Of the original eight subspecies, at least three are now extinct. Little is known of these populations beyond a handful of rare photographs and

museum specimens left in existence today. The Caspian, also known locally as the Hyrcanian or Turan tiger, once roamed across Turkey, Iran, Iraq, Afghanistan, Mongolia, and the central Asiatic area of Russia. Much of this habitat was quite arid and therefore unique to this tiger subspecies. The Caspian also differed from other tigers in that it followed prey, such as boars, on their migrations instead of holding territories all year round as other tigers do. (Having said this, there is evidence that some Amur tigers also followed prey migrations, until these were disrupted by overhunting.) The demise of the Caspian tigers began in the early twentieth century, when the Russian government ordered its army to kill them in order to free up land for cultivation. The soldiers soon pushed the last remaining tigers into the mountain forests, where they found life more difficult. The last certain sighting of a Caspian tiger was in the 1950s. Although it is now extinct, it is still regarded as one of the three subspecies—the West Asian tiger—according to the new classification.

The Balinese tiger, from the island of Bali in Indonesia, was the smallest subspecies, being only half the size of the Amur or Siberian tiger. It was dark with many thin stripes, much like the Sumatran and Javan tigers. As it was confined to a tiny island and suffered from speedily increasing human populations, the Balinese tiger was the first to become extinct. It had vanished by the early 1930s.

The Javan tiger was, as the name suggests, found solely on the island of Java, which at 132,000 sq km is just over one-quarter the size of Sumatra. The Javan looked very much like the Sunda Island tiger, with thin dark stripes, which were often double-looped. Another distinctive feature was its long cheek whiskers. Until the early nineteenth century, Javan tigers were common, but like the Caspian they were exterminated as people continued to expand their agricultural lands. As Java became exceptionally densely populated, the Javan tiger, not surprisingly, became the most recent known extinction, sometime in the 1970s. Both the Javan and the Balinese tigers are regarded as a part of the Sunda Island subspecies in the new classification.

There are sporadic reports of all three of these extinct tigers being spotted in the wild, but none has been professionally validated or backed up with photographic or other hard evidence. It is assumed that most of these possible sightings were of leopards or other big cats.

Tiger and leopard skins seized from a truck in Ghaziabad, UP, revealing a sharp acceleration in the trade.

India's Tigers: On the Brink of Extinction?

There has never been a century like the twenty-first for the tiger. It is vanishing rapidly from many of its habitats. I never thought to live through a year such as 2005. From 2004 to 2005 the report card shows total disaster. At least eighty tigers from just seven protected areas are gone— probably poached. If counts were done for the other seventy-five protected areas also, the toll would surely be appalling. Tragically, this year showed beyond doubt that the Royal Bengal tiger is on the verge of extinction. In late 2004-early 2005 a local extinction of tigers from Sariska Tiger Reserve in Rajasthan came to light. In the same year came the confirmation of a sharp drop in the tiger population of Ranthambhore National Park (at least twenty-one tigers are missing), a Project Tiger reserve. By 2005 Panna Tiger Reserve in Madhya Pradesh lost at least twenty tigers. In 2006 there were reports of the recovery of three freshly poached tiger skins from Periyar Tiger Reserve, where a huge farcical exercise of rehabilitating poachers in the role of 'protectors' has been undertaken. The area around the Sundarbans has also seen the seizure of skins, there have been a couple of seizures in Orissa and UP, and a haul of five tiger skins and thirty-eight leopard skins on the borders of Nepal and Tibet. Poaching is rampant. And all this is going on in and around Project Tiger reserves. The sorry state of affairs in the area outside our premier parks can only be imagined. And we are not even talking of Manas, Indrawati, Nagarjunasagar, Palamau, Valmiki, Dampha, Namdapha, and Buxa—all tiger reserves that are plagued by a severe set of problems. Smaller sanctuaries like Kela Devi, Sawai Man Singh, Palpurkuno, and Rani Durgawati have lost all their tigers recently.

There have been other moments in the past when the tiger in India has been threatened. The tiger as a trophy has always been valued, and its very abundance in the past has spelt terrible excesses against it. Hunting records of Indian princes and the British in India make for grim reading. But the tiger survived unlike the cheetah.

At two other moments in India's history as an independent nation, the tiger faced a severe crisis. The first

A tiger with its leg caught in a vicious trap.

was tided over by concerned, capable, and decisive political leadership at
the helm of affairs. It in fact saw the genesis of Project Tiger in 1973—the
only proud moment in independent India's tiger conservation history. The
second crisis in 1992 bears uncanny and disheartening similarity to the
present one in terms of causes, and delayed and defensive official
responses and reactions focused on cover-up rather than positive action.

Its use in Chinese medicine and Tibetan ceremonial costumes has
replaced trophy hunting as the most potent threat to the tiger in recent
years, and organized and armed poaching and smuggling gangs with
international links operate fearlessly in many of our national parks. The
time has come for immediate and drastic action if we are to save this
majestic animal, and I fear it may already be too late. The government has
ignored the numerous warnings like an ostrich burying its head in the
sand, and we now have a full-blown and, I'm afraid, terminal crisis on our
hands. Even now, when drastic surgical measures are called for, the
government is opting for weak populist measures that will leave us, I have
no hesitation in declaring, a tigerless nation, with future generations

holding us accountable for the mass murder of this proud and beautiful animal. The Prime Minister, at last recognizing the enormity of the problem, constituted a Tiger Task Force to deal with the problem in 2005, but unfortunately most of its members had no experience of wild tigers. Although I too was a member, I was outvoted by these people who couldn't see the gravity of the situation. They pushed for a people-centric approach when it is only too clear from the huge spate of recent poaching cases, in all of which local tribal populations have been hugely involved, that people and tigers cannot coexist. In the past too successes like Ranthambhore and Kanha were created only by relocating the villages that used to exist inside the boundaries of the parks.

The fashions of today are about sharing power and co-managing natural resources. Can this be done with the rampant corruption that has percolated every strata of our society?

Why is it so difficult to reach an agreement with all the parties that 50,000 sq km of habitat must be inviolate for 2000 plus tigers to live and breed in? This is what tigers need. Their biology demands undisturbed habitats to breed in. The tiger areas need to be sealed forever. This is not a matter for debate. Tigers need inviolate spaces away from the crazy world of so-called sensitive human beings.

Forest guards and police with tiger bones recovered from poachers.

Legislations like the Tribal Bill (Recognition of Rights of both Tribal and Forest Dwellers) which will award forest land to hundreds of thousands of families will ring the death knell for tigers. Tigers do not breed in coexistence with human beings. They need inviolate spaces, and so do the deer and the boar and the gaur. These are the prey of the tiger that eat grass and grow in population, and then the tiger has enough of a prey base to increase its population. It is these basic essentials that must be understood by human rights activists. It is then that tiger populations rise or are maintained at healthy levels. If people are not prepared to relocate, we may need to relocate tigers so they can be saved.

If we track back to the 1970s, the early tiger reserves were full of villages, be it in Ranthambhore, or Kanha, or Corbett, or any other area. We know that after many of the villages were relocated, ungulates flourished and tiger numbers also shot up. By the late 1980s, the tiger population had risen to 4000 from 1800 in the early 1970s.

From 1975 to 2005 I have followed the story of Ranthambhore's tigers. I have witnessed the population rising from 12 to 14, when I first went there, to 50 in 1987. This is fact not fiction, and it is all due to village relocation. There are enough records that prove the same from Nagarahole in the south to Manas in the north-east. Human activity destroys tiger habitats, and in 2007 the population dynamics are such that the tiger has no chance. As areas get more and more disturbed the tiger vanishes, as we have seen in Sariska. And there are many more Sariskas waiting to happen. Some have already happened.

Writing in 1978 of a Sariska that was still a haven for the tiger and his prey, Kailash Sankhala, one of our foremost foresters, could already see the danger signals. Alas! they were not heeded and the shame of Sariska 2005 happened.

A tigress and her cub watch from the cover of high grass.

Waiting for the Tiger

Kailash Sankhala

On one occasion as I waited in my hide near a water hole in Sariska, hopes rose with the alarm call of a sambar. At that moment the silence and darkness were shattered by a distant flashing of lights and with it my hopes disappeared. A minibus rolled in with a load of talkative tourists. Jai Singh, the game warden, had promised them a glimpse of a tiger and, failing to find one, he flashed his spotlight on my hide. He started talking about my research and told his audience about how I would spend a cold night in the company of tigers without any weapons. Some wondered, some pitied, while others wished me luck. Mercifully the warden did not know about the alarm call so they left me to it, and I cursed them for ruining my chances. …

We welcome disciplined tourists and those who are really interested in the wildlife, but many merely want to add the tiger to their list with the temples and the Taj. An influx of non-serious tourists is not what our reserves need. …

On another occasion in, May 1971, I had spent the day in the same hide at Sariska. Evening fell and I was watching a bait when a tiger arrived. He lowered his body and rushed at the victim. There was a choked bellow, and the tiger stood motionless with the head of the calf in his mouth. I could hear his heavy breathing, and after 20 seconds he opened his jaws and the lifeless body fell down with a thud. For a minute the tiger stood still, then walked away, completely unconcerned, for a drink. After ten minutes I heard the repeated calls of a lapwing. The tiger came back to the kill, gave a few tugs, and dragged the carcass a short distance. Next I heard the sound of tearing skin and the crushing of bones.

These sounds were clearly heard by some sambar hinds and a stag, who stood on the shore barely 45 ft from the tiger. They were nervous, but this did not prevent the stag from drinking for two minutes, pausing for a few seconds and drinking again, after which he trotted off. Similarly some chital drank and went away, and finally a porcupine arrived and was quite unconcerned. The tiger, busy munching, paid no attention to the juicy prey within his reach. Recently, in May 1977, at Sariska, I saw a sambar doe and two fawns sitting in an ash-patch absolutely unconcerned while a tigress and her grown-up cub fed in full view hardly a hundred yards or so away. Even when my jeep disturbed the tigers and they moved away, this did not bother the sambar. Animals know that the tiger, unlike man, is satisfied with what he has killed for the day and is not concerned with tomorrow. He takes only what he needs and does not kill for the sake of killing. There is a perfect understanding between predator and prey. For the first time I felt ashamed of being a man, who is not trusted even by the jackals, much less the deer and antelopes. …

By photographing and taking notes over long periods of time in some places I came to know the animals and birds almost by name, or at least by their morphological peculiarities such as deformities, injuries, and battle scars. …

Although I identified with these creatures they never trusted me: the understanding was all one-sided. Even my scent sends them bolting. I have wondered whether it was my fault, but then I tell myself that it is nothing personal but an inbuilt fear of man which the animals have developed because human action has exceeded the natural limits of predation. Man is the embodiment of unpredictable danger, so I could never be accepted as part of the ecology of tigerland and can only remain a secret witness to the animals' lives.

Kailash Sankhala (1925–94) was the director of Delhi Zoological Park and Chief Wildlife Warden of Rajasthan. Well known around the world as the 'Tiger Man' for his work in preserving tigers, he was involved in the formation of Project Tiger, the world's largest wildlife conservation programme set up in India in 1973. This extract has been taken from *Tiger! The Story of the Indian Tiger*, first published in 1978.

Who would believe that right next to Delhi and Jaipur we lost an entire population of tigers—a national shame for which no one has been held accountable.

So what do we need to do?

We have 100–120,000 sq km with some evidence of tigers. This could be reduced and probably will fall drastically because of neglect. It is still only 5 per cent of the forest area of India. We could decide that we want 50,000 sq km or more of habitat for tigers. We already have 34,000 sq km in our tiger reserves. This could look after 2000 plus tigers if we are lucky. We must then make sure that all the villages inside are relocated by giving the people the best possible deals. This habitat must then be managed by hand-picked men from the Indian Forest Service—and hand picked down to rangers, foresters, and forest guards. Something on these lines exists in Kanha and Kaziranga. The job at hand is to protect the tiger's turf like never before. In this mission, the fringe-area population can be engaged in protection, water and soil conservation, and other forest-related jobs. This is how local people will play a role in keeping tiger habitats inviolate. This will play a role in creating and increasing forest wealth. Income generation can take place from tourism when permitted. The locals need to participate with the management in the day-to-day decision-making process in order to keep the area disturbance free, but the focus has to be on protection not exploitation.

This is where the challenge lies.

If we don't succeed in relocating villages, then the inviolate areas will reduce. I believe the job at hand will be to pick up all the stray tigers and relocate them to the remnants of inviolate areas or well protected areas. Here they will at least live for a while. Look at the example of the tiger that strayed into Bharatpur—it survived peacefully for more then 5 years amongst the birds and the deer. It is quite clear that when political will does not allow for relocating people, we will have to find a way to relocate tigers before they all die the most hideous of deaths at the hands of man.

Conclusion

The tiger's future is entirely dependent on it being left alone by human beings. It will only survive away from human presence. The role of human beings is to create and protect inviolate tiger habitats. In 2007 I do not see this happening in a country of 1.2 billion people. The leadership of this country just doesn't have the political will to do this. In fact new populist legislation is doing just the opposite—providing our forests to people with the rationale that tigers and people can coexist.

The Tiger Task Force report resulted in the creation of a Tiger Conservation Authority, but ironically, though created for the tiger, the majority of its members are 'people' activists and representatives of scheduled tribes and other groups. Even the so-called wildlife experts in this group of twenty-odd people have little experience of wild tigers. This is the new authority that has replaced Project Tiger after 34 years and, needless to say, there is little that can be hoped for from this disparate group with everybody following different agendas, none of which seems to be tiger-centric. The federal arm of governance dealing with wildlife and forests has never been in a worse mess than in 2006–7. For more than six months the positions of DG Forests and Additional DG Wildlife have been vacant, and the National Board of Wildlife and Forest Advisory Committee have largely been defunct.

The only out-of-the-box solution seems to lie in relocating tigers from problem- and conflict-ridden areas to relatively safer and more protected areas like Corbett, Kanha, Kaziranga, Sunderbans, Nagarahole, and Bandipur. In some cases they can even be shifted to vast captive enclosures so that they are at least free of the danger of poachers' traps, poison, and bullets.

I can think of no other tiger-friendly solution in this atmosphere of uninformed and indifferent leadership and officials.

Project Tiger Reserves in India

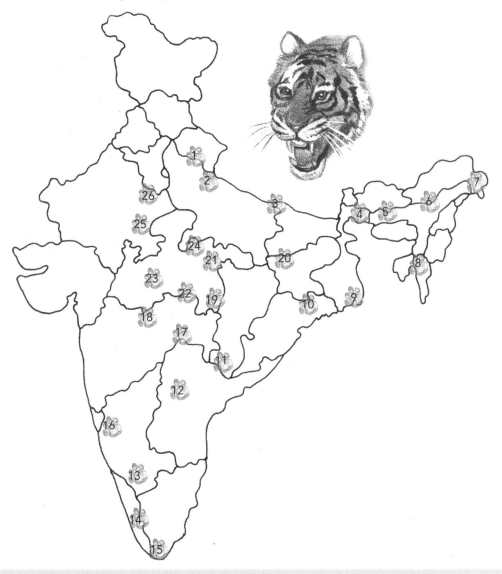

1. Corbett (Uttaranchal)	10. Simlipal (Orissa)	18. Melghat (Maharashtra)
2. Dudhwa (Uttar Pradesh)	11. Indrawati (Chhattisgarh)	19. Kanha (Madhya Pradesh)
3. Valmiki (Bihar)	12. Nagarjunasagar (Andhra	20. Palamau (Jharkhand)
4. Buxa (West Bengal)	Pradesh)	21. Bandhavgarh (Madhya Pradesh)
5. Manas (Assam)	13. Bandipur (Karnataka)	22. Pench (Madhya Pradesh &
6. Pakhui-Nameri (Arunachal	14. Periyar (Kerala)	Maharashtra)
Pradesh)	15. Kalakad-Mundanthurai (Tamil	23. Bori-Satpura (Madhya Pradesh)
7. Namdapha (Arunachal Pradesh)	Nadu)	24. Panna (Madhya Pradesh)
8. Dampha (Mizoram)	16. Bhadra (Karnataka)	25. Ranthambhore (Rajasthan)
9. Sundarbans (West Bengal)	17. Tadoba-Andhari (Maharashtra)	26. Sariska (Rajasthan)

Please note: Till November 2006, a total of 36 Project Tiger Reserves had been notified all across India. These include Nagarahole in Karnataka, Madumalai in Tamil Nadu, Kaziranga in Assam, Satkosia in Orissa, Achanakmar, Sitanadi, and Udanti in Chhattisgarh, and Sanjay in Madhya Pradesh.